BELIEF AND UNBELIEF

Discussions and Comparisons

THE RISALE-I NUR COLLECTION

BELIEF AND UNBELIEF

Discussions and Comparisons

BEDIÜZZAMAN SAİD NURSİ

Translated by
Hüseyin Akarsu

New Jersey

Published by The Light, Inc.
345 Clifton Ave., Clifton,
NJ, 07011, USA

www.thelightpublishing.com

Library of Congress Cataloging-in-Publication Data Available

ISBN 978-1-59784-265-6 (hardcover)

Printed by
Numune Matbaacılık ve Cilt San. Ltd. Şti. Istanbul - Turkey
www.numune.com.tr

Table of Contents

Preface

COMPARISONS BETWEEN BELIEF AND UNBELIEF IS ONE OF THE important books among the *Risale-i Nur* Collection which is composed of the *risales* (epistles) in which unbelief and unbelief are compared in concrete terms. The *Risale-i Nur* Collection comprises the works of Bediüzzaman Said Nursi (1877–1960), who, being one of the most effective and profound representatives of Islam's intellectual, moral, and spiritual strengths, launched an overall revival of Islam in the second quarter of the twentieth century in Turkey. He spent his life overflowing with love and ardor for Islam, pursuing a wise and measured activism based on sound reasoning, and following the Qur'an and the Prophetic example.

The *Risale-i Nur* explains Islam and belief to modern people in their own terms and addressing their modern minds. Analyzing both belief and unbelief, he used clearly reasoned arguments to prove the essentials of Islamic faith and explain the meaning and importance of worshipping God in human life.

Using easily understood stories, comparisons, and explanations, Said Nursi produced categorical proofs showing that modern scientific discoveries actually support and reinforce the truths of the Religion. He used the Qur'anic methodology of addressing each person's intellect, and all inner and outer facilities, to encourage people to study the universe and its functioning in order to understand creation's true nature and purposes. This, in turn, leads to learning the One Creator's Attributes and their own duties as God's servants.

Said Nursi explained the universe's true nature as being a comprehensive sign of its Creator, and showed via clear arguments that all fundamentals of belief can be proven rationally when the universe is read in this way. As belief is then grounded in modern science, it remains firm and immune to materialism, naturalism, and atheism.

Such believers view all scientific and technological advances as merely uncovering the cosmos' workings. Viewing the cosmos as a vast and infinitely complex and meaningful unified book describing its Single Author, all discoveries and advances reinforce, deepen, and expand belief. Thus their most fundamental needs—to worship God by recognizing His Most Beautiful Names and Attributes, and to obey His laws—are met.

Said Nursi himself describes the *Risale-i Nur* as a true commentary on the wise Qur'an that emanates from its miraculousness. In addition to proving the six pillars of Islamic belief through both concrete and rational arguments and producing the human conscience and basic nature as witnesses, especially through comparisons it vividly demonstrates the true natures of and difference between belief and unbelief. It demonstrates that in misguidance there is a sort of Hell in this world as well, while in belief there is a kind of Paradise. It shows the severe pains in sins, evil deeds, and forbidden pleasures, and proves that pleasures akin to those in Paradise are to be found in good deeds and virtues, and in the truths of the Religion.

The following question was asked about the *Risale-i Nur*: "Why is it that despite the ongoing violent attacks of its malicious, obdurate opponents against it and their vicious treatment of it, and despite their shameful lies and propaganda against it to destroy it and to scare people away from it, the *Risale-i Nur* spreads in an unprecedented way and causes itself to be read with great enthusiasm both within the country and abroad, conquering people's minds and hearts?" The answer that was given is as if it was describing *Comparisons between Belief and Unbelief*. It is as follows:

> Being a true commentary on the wise Qur'an based on its miraculousness or inimitability, the *Risale-i Nur* demonstrates that there is in misguidance a sort of Hell in this world as well, while in belief there is a sort of Paradise. It points out the grievous pains in sins, evil deeds, and forbidden pleasures, and demonstrates that in good deeds and virtues and the truths of the Religion are to be found pleasures like the pleasures of Paradise. In this way it saves the sensible among those who have fallen into vice and misguidance. For at this time there are two terrible realities:
>
> THE FIRST: Since human emotions, which are blind to the consequences of things and prefer an ounce of immediate pleasure to tons of future joy, have come to prevail over mind and reason, the only way to save the dissipated from their vices is to show them the pain which underlies their apparent pleasures and thus defeat their emotions. As indicated by the verse, *They choose the present, worldly life over the Hereafter* (14:3), even those who believe and are aware to

certain extents of the diamond-like bounties and pleasures of the Hereafter tend to prefer worldly pleasures, which are like pieces of glass destined soon to shatter over them. Therefore, the only way to save the people (of belief or unbelief) from following the people of misguidance on account of this reality and love for the world is by showing them the hellish torments and pains present in the way of misguidance. This is the method the *Risale-i Nur* follows. For at this time, in the face of the obduracy coming from absolute unbelief and the misguidance caused by scientific materialism or scientism and the addiction to vice, only one in ten or even twenty can be turned away from vice and encouraged to give it up by proving the existence of Hell and its torments, after having given them certain amount of knowledge of God the Almighty. However, even after they have received this instruction, it is still possible that such people will say: "God is the All-Forgiving and the All-Compassionate, and Hell is a long way off," and continue in their dissipation. Their hearts and spirits are defeated by their emotions.

Thus, by showing through most of its comparisons between belief and unbelief the grievous and terrifying results in this world of unbelief and misguidance, the *Risale-i Nur* causes even the most stubborn and arrogant people to feel repugnance with regard to those inauspicious, illicit pleasures, thus leading them to repent. The short comparisons in the Sixth, Seventh, and Eighth Words, and the long one in The Third Station of The Thirty-Second Word frighten the most dissipated and misguided person away from the way they are following, leading them to accept what is taught. As an example, I will relate briefly the states that the Verse of Light (24:35)—which beings with *God is the Light of the heavens and the earth*—showed me on a journey of the imagination, which were in fact reality. Those who desire a detailed account of it may refer to the end of *Sikke-i Tasdik-i Gaybi* ("The Confirming Stamp of the Unseen").

During that imaginary journey I saw the animal kingdom in need of provision, and I looked upon it through the prism of materialist philosophy. Their weakness and impotence in the face of their innumerable needs and severe hunger showed that kingdom to be a most miserable and painful one. Since I was looking with the eyes of the people of misguidance and heedlessness, I cried out. Then suddenly I saw through the telescope of Qur'anic wisdom and belief that the Divine Name the All-Merciful had risen in the sign of the All-Providing like a shining sun, gilding that hungry, wretched animal world with the light of its mercy.

Then I saw within the animal world another wretched realm which was enveloped in darkness and where the young were struggling in their need and powerlessness. It was enough to make anyone feel pity. I regretted having looked with the eyes of the people of misguidance. Suddenly, belief gave me different spectacles and I saw the Name the All-Compassionate rise in the sign of affection and tenderness. It changed that painful world into a joyful one in such a beautiful and lovable fashion and illuminated it in such a way that my tears of complaint and sorrow were transformed into tears of rejoice and thanks.

Then the world of humanity appeared to me as though on a cinema screen. Looking again through the telescope of the people of misguidance, I saw that world to be so dark and terrifying that I cried out from the depths of my heart. Human beings have desires and ambitions that extend to eternity; they have thoughts and conceptions that encompass the entire universe and earnest desires and yearnings for eternal life, everlasting happiness, and Paradise. They have innate capacities and powers that are unrestricted and left free. Also, despite their weakness, impotence, and very brief life, they have innumerable needs and purposes, and are exposed to the attacks of countless adversaries and the blows of endless calamities. Under the perpetual threat of death, they are leading a brief and tumultuous life in wretched circumstances. Striving for their livelihood in misery and suffering from the continuous blows of death and separation—a most painful and terrifying state for the heart and conscience—they are heading straight for the grave, which appears to the misguided to be the door to everlasting darkness. I saw that they are being cast individually and in groups into that well of darkness.

On seeing the world of humanity under such layers of darkness I was just about to cry out with my heart, spirit, and mind, indeed, with all my faculties and even all the particles of my being, when the light and power of belief issuing from the Qur'an smashed these spectacles of misguidance, providing me with a different means of vision. I saw God's Name the All-Just rise like the sun in the sign of the All-Wise, the Name the All-Merciful in the sign of the All-Munificent, the Name the All-Compassionate in the sign of the All-Forgiving, the Name the All-Resurrecting in the sign of the All-Inheriting, the Name the All-Reviving in the sign of the All-Favoring, and the name the All-Nurturing in the sign of the Sovereign. They lit up that entire dark world of humanity, within which there are many other worlds. They dispelled these hellish states and, opening up windows from the luminous worlds of the Hereafter, scattered light over the world of humanity. I uttered: "All praise and gratitude be to God; thanks be to God to the number of particles in existence!" I saw and knew to the degree of certainty arising from vision that in belief there is a sort of Paradise in this world too, while in misguidance there is a kind of Hell.

Then the realm of the earth appeared. On that journey of the imagination, the dark, hypothetical rules of the philosophy and laws of the science which do not obey the Religion presented an appalling world to my imagination. Voyaging through space on the ship of the extremely ancient earth—which travels in a year the distance that it would take a human being twenty-five thousand years to walk, with a movement seventy times faster than a cannon-ball, and being a structure that could break up at any moment with the innermost parts being in constant flux and turmoil—wretched humankind appeared to be trapped in a most desolate darkness. I became dizzy and almost lost self-control. I flung the spectacles of philosophy to the ground, smashing them. Then, suddenly, I looked with a view illuminated by the wisdom of the Qur'an and belief. I saw the Names the Creator of the heavens and earth, the All-Powerful, the All-Knowing Nurturer, God, the Lord of the heavens and earth, and the Subjugator of the sun and moon rise like suns in the signs of Mercy, Grandeur and Lordship. They illuminated that dark, desolate, and terrifying world with such brilliance that the earth appeared to the eye of my belief as a perfectly well-ordered, subservient, pleasant, and safe vessel in which the provisions of everyone have been stored. I saw it as a ship or an airplane or a train which has been prepared for trade and enjoyment, carrying beings with spirits through the Lord's realms around the sun, bringing the produce of spring, summer, and fall to those in need of sustenance. I exclaimed: "All praise and gratitude be to God to the number of the atoms of the earth for the favor of belief!"

It has thus been proved with many examples and analogies in the *Risale-i Nur* that the people of vice and misguidance suffer a hellish torment in this world too, while on account of the manifestations of belief, the people of faith and righteousness can taste paradisiacal pleasures through the stomachs of Islam and humanity. They are able to benefit, each according to the degree of their belief. But in these stormy times, the currents numb the senses and scatter human attention to peripheral, futile matters and engulf them, anesthetizing their senses, obliterating sound reasoning and reflection. As a result, the people of misguidance are temporarily unable to totally perceive their spiritual torment, while the people of guidance are overwhelmed by heedlessness and cannot truly appreciate the pleasures of right guidance.

THE SECOND TERRIBLE REALITY OF THIS AGE: Compared with today, in former times there was little misguidance that arose from absolute unbelief and blind faith in science, and little obstinacy that emanated from stubborn, willful unbelief. For this reason, the teaching and arguments of the religious scholars of those times were enough to dispel any unbelief arising from doubt. Since almost everyone believed in God, most people would give up misguidance and vice after being taught about God and warned about Hell-fire. But now there are a hundred absolute unbelievers in one small town, when in the past there was only one. Those who go astray due to blind faith in science and learning, obstinately opposing the truths of belief, are a hundred times greater in number in relation to former times. As these obstinate deniers oppose the truths of belief with the arrogance of the Pharaoh, there must be a sacred truth that will utterly destroy the foundations of their unbelief in this world with the strength of an atomic explosion, halting their aggression and bringing some of them to belief.

Endless thanks be to God Almighty that with its numerous comparisons and the remedies it provides for the ills of this time, the *Risale-i Nur*, which comprises some gleams of the Qur'an of miraculous exposition, vanquishes even the worst of those obstinate deniers with the diamond sword of the Qur'an. By indicating the proofs and arguments for Divine Unity and the truths of belief that exist to the number of the atoms of the universe, for twenty-five years it has not been defeated in the face of the severest attacks; indeed it has been victorious. With its comparisons of belief and unbelief, of right guidance and misguidance, the *Risale-i Nur* self-evidently proves these truths. For example, if one looks at the proofs and gleams in The Second Station of The Twenty-Second Word, The First Station of The Thirty-Second Word, the "Windows" of The Thirty-Third Word, and the eleven proofs of The Staff of Moses (*Asa-yi Musa*), and if other comparisons are considered in their light, it can be understood that it is the truths of the Qur'an that are manifested in the *Risale-i Nur* which will smash and destroy absolute unbelief and obdurate misguidance at this time.

Comparisons between Belief and Unbelief is composed of the most of the comparisons that are mentioned in the answer above. All other books of the *Risale-i Nur* Collection with the exception of few have been translated into English and published by the Tughra Books. They are as follows:

The Words – The Reconstruction of Islamic Belief and Thought

The Letters – Epistles on Islamic Thought, Belief, and Life

The Gleams – Reflections on Qur'anic Wisdom and Spirituality

The Rays – Reflections on Islamic Belief, Thought, Worship, and Action

Al-Mathnawi an-Nuri – Seedbed of the *Light*

The Staff of Moses – Reflections on Islamic Faith, and Divine Existence and Unity

The Reasonings – A Key to Understanding the Qur'anic Eloquence

Gleams of Truth – Prescriptions for a Healthy Social Life

The Publisher

The First Word

The worth of Bismillah

In the Name of God, the All-Merciful, the All-Compassionate.

ISMILLAH (IN THE NAME OF GOD) IS THE START OF ALL GOOD things, so we will start with it. This blessed phrase is a mark of Islam, one constantly recited by all creatures through their tongues of disposition. If you want to perceive its inexhaustible source of strength and blessing, consider the following parable:

Travelers in a desert where uncivilized people live must travel under a tribal chief's name and protection, or else they will be bothered by bandits and unable to acquire what they need for the journey. Two people, one humble and the other arrogant, set out on a journey. The humble one obtained the name of a tribal chief; the arrogant one did not. The former traveled everywhere in safety. Whenever he met a bandit, he said: "I'm travelling in the name of such-and-such tribal chief," and so was left alone. He was treated with respect in every tent he entered. In contrast, the arrogant one suffered disaster and constant fear, for he had to struggle and beg for every need. He became base and vile.

O arrogant soul! You are that traveler, and this world is the desert. Your weakness and poverty are endless, and the enemies and privations to which you are exposed are beyond number. Given this, invoke the name of the Eternal Owner and the Everlasting Ruler of this world, for only this can deliver you from such begging and fear.

Bismillah is a blessed treasure. It transforms your boundless weakness and poverty, by binding you to the All-Powerful and Merciful One's infinite Power and Mercy, into the most heeded intercessor at His Exalted Court. When you say *bismillah*, you act in His Name. You are like a soldier acting in the state's name, fearing no one, doing all things in the name of the law and the state, and persisting against all odds.

How does everything recite *bismillah* through its very mode of existence? For example: A stranger arriving in a city can order its people to gather at a certain place to work on a certain task. If this order is obeyed, the stranger obviously is acting in the name of the ruler's strength and authority, not his own. In the same way, everything acts in the name of God, the All-Mighty. Small seeds and grains carry huge trees on their heads and raise weights as heavy as mountains. Each tree says *bismillah* and, filling its hands with fruit from Mercy's treasury, offers them to us on a tray. Each garden, a cooking pot from the Divine Power's kitchen where countless varieties of delicious foods are prepared, says *bismillah*.

All blessed animals (e.g., cows, camels, sheep, and goats) say *bismillah* and become fountains of milk from Mercy's abundance. They offer us, in the All-Providing's Name, a most delicate and pure food like the water of life. Every plant and blade of grass, every root and stem, says *bismillah*. All plant, tree, and grass roots and fibers, soft as silk, say *bismillah* and pierce hard stones and soil. Mentioning His Name, the Name of the All-Merciful, subjects everything to them.

A tree's branches spread in the sky, and its roots spread unhindered in hard rocks and soil. Some plants yield fruit underground, and delicate, green leaves hold moisture despite intense heat for a long time. These realities vex the naturalist. They jab a finger into the naturalist's unseeing eye and say: "You put so much trust in the power of hardness and heat, yet they obey the Divine Command. That is why each soft fiber of the plant's roots, like Moses' staff, obeys: *And We said: 'Strike the rock with your staff!'* (2:60) and penetrates the rock. Every delicate, paper-thin leaf, like the members of Prophet Abraham's body, recites: *O fire, be coolness and peace!* (21:69) in defiance of the intense heat.

All things inwardly say *bismillah* and deliver God's bounties to us in His Name. Thus we also should say *bismillah*, give and take in His Name, and accept nothing from those who do not give in God's Name.

QUESTION: We pay people for whatever they bring us, even though they are only "tray-bearers." What payment does God, their true Owner, ask of us?

ANSWER: That true Bestower of all precious bounties and goods we enjoy requires three things: remembrance, thanksgiving, and reflection. Saying *bismillah* at the beginning is a manner of remembrance, and saying *al-hamdu li'llah* (All praise and gratitude are for God) at their end is a manner of thanksgiving. Reflection means always being mindful and thinking of the precious and ingenious bounties we receive as miracles of the Eternally Besought One's Power and as gifts from His Mercy.

If you kissed the hand of someone who brought you a precious gift without recognizing the true sender (the king), you would be making a great mistake. Praising and loving the apparent bestower of bounty, while forgetting the true Bestower of bounty, is far worse. O soul! If you wish to avoid such stupidity, give and receive in God's Name. Begin and act, to the very end, in His Name. This is the kernel of the matter.

The Second Word

The way to contentment

In the Name of God, the All-Merciful, the All-Compassionate.

Those who believe in the Unseen (2:2)

IF YOU WISH TO UNDERSTAND HOW TO ENJOY GREAT CONTENTMENT and blessing through belief, and how to experience fulfillment and ease, consider the following parable:

Two people travel for both pleasure and business. The first one is conceited and pessimistic, and so ends up in what he considers a most wicked country. He sees himself surrounded by poor and hopeless people tormented by bullies and living ruined lives. He sees the same grievous, painful situation wherever he goes, as if the whole country were a house of mourning. In order not to feel this painful situation, he finds no other way out than becoming drunk. Everyone seems to him to be an enemy and foreigner. He has awful visions of corpses and orphans, and his soul is plunged into torment.

The second person, a God-serving, decent, and fair-minded man, goes to a country that he considers quite excellent. Seeing a universal festival, he finds joy and happiness in every corner, and a house for remembering God overflowing with rapture. Everyone is a loving friend, even a relative, to him. He sees the celebrations of a general discharge from duties accompanied by cries of good wishes and thanks. Hearing a drum and a band for enlisting soldiers with happy calls of "God is the All-Great" and "There is no deity but God," he becomes happy at his own joy and that of others. He enjoys a comfortable trade and thanks God.

When he returns after some while, he meets the other man, understands his situation and says: "You've become crazy. The bad and ugly things you see come from and reflect your inner world. You imagine laughter to be weeping, and discharge from duties to be sack and pillage. Come to your senses and clean your heart, so that this inauspicious veil will be raised from your eyes and you may see the truth. This is an orderly, prosperous, and civilized country with a powerful, compassionate, and just ruler. So things cannot be as you see or think." The man comes to his senses and is full of regret: "Yes, I've really gone crazy because of all those intoxicants. Thank you. May God be pleased with you for rescuing me from such a hellish state."

O my soul! The first person represents an unbeliever or a heedless sinner who sees this world as a place of general mourning, all living things as weeping orphans due to the pain of separation and decay, people and animals as lonely and uncivilized creatures cut down by death, and great masses (mountains and oceans) as terrible corpses without souls. His unbelief and misguidance breed great anxieties that torture him.

The second person believes in and affirms God Almighty. He sees the world as a place where people glorify, praise and exalt Him, a practice arena for people and animals, and an examination hall for people and jinn. Animals and humanity are demobilized so that after death believers can travel in spiritual enjoyment to the other world—for this world needs a new generation to populate and work in it.

All animals and people enter this world for a reason. All living things are as soldiers or officials, happy with their appointed task. The sound we hear is their praise and glorifying as they begin, or their pleasure while working, or their thanksgiving as they finish. Believers see all things as obedient servants, friendly officials, a lovable book of their All-Munificent Master and All-Compassionate Owner.

Many more such beautiful, sublime, and pleasurable truths arise from belief. This is because belief bears the seed of what is, in effect, a Touba tree of Paradise, whereas unbelief contains the seed of a Zaqqum tree of Hell. Safety and well-being are found only in Islam (submission to God) and belief. Therefore, always thank God, saying: "Praise be to God for Islam and perfect belief."

The Third Word

Choosing the right way

In the Name of God, the All-Merciful, the All-Compassionate.

O you people, worship… (2:21)

F YOU WISH TO UNDERSTAND THE BLISS AND BENEFIT THAT COME with worship, and the loss and destruction that come with vice, dissipation, and ignoring God's commands, consider the following parable: Two soldiers are told to go to a far town. Travelling together, they come to a fork and meet a wise person who tells them: "The road on the right is risk-free, and nine out of ten travelers meet with great advantage but no harm. The road on the left offers no benefit, and nine out of ten travelers suffer great loss. Both roads are of the same length. But there is one difference: Those who take the left road, which has no rules or someone in charge, travel without equipment or arms, and so appear comfortable and at ease. Those who take the right road, which is under military order, carry their own food in a kit-bag, and a heavy weapon which will overpower and rout every enemy."

One soldier takes the right fork. Shouldering his heavy load, his heart and soul are simultaneously freed of any burdensome debt and fear. Travelling in peace, he reaches his destination, where he receives a reward worthy of an honest soldier who fully performs his duties. The other soldier takes the left fork. Carrying nothing heavy, his heart and soul nevertheless suffer from innumerable dangers and anxieties. He is constantly fearful and in need. When he reaches the destined town, he is treated as a rebel and fugitive.

Now, my undisciplined and carnal soul, pay attention. The first soldier represents an obedient servant of God; the second soldier represents rebels and those who follow their own desire. The road is the lifeline coming from the world of spirits, passing through this world and the grave, and continuing toward the Hereafter.

The heavy load and weapon are worship and piety. Worship seems to be a strenuous demand, but in reality gives indescribable peace and comfort. Those who pray recite *Ashhadu an la ilaha illa'llah* (I bear witness that there is no deity but God), the Creator and the All-Providing. Only He can give harm and benefit. He is the All-Wise Who does nothing useless, the All-Compassionate Whose mercy and bounty are abundant. Having belief, the believing soldier sees in every event a door to the wealth of God's Mercy and knocks on it via prayer and supplication. Realizing that his Lord and Sustainer controls everything, he takes refuge in Him. Putting his trust in and fully submitting to God, he resists evil. His belief gives him complete confidence.

As with every good action, courage arises from belief in and loyal devotion to God as well. As with every bad action, cowardice arises from misguidance. If the earth were to explode, those servants of God with truly illuminated hearts would not frightened—they might even consider it a marvel of the Eternally Besought One's Power. A rationalist but unbelieving philosopher might tremble at the sight of a comet, lest it should strike the earth. (This was how some Americans reacted to the recent sighting of Halley's comet.)

Our ability to meet our endless demands is negligible. We are threatened with afflictions that our own strength cannot withstand. Our strength is limited to what we can reach, yet our wishes and demands, suffering and sorrow, are as wide as our imagination.

Anyone not wholly blind to the truth understands that our best option is to submit to God, to worship, believe, and have confidence in Him. A safe road is preferable to a dangerous one, even one with a very low probability of safe passage. The way of belief certainly leads one safely to endless bliss; the way of unbelief and transgression, meanwhile, is not profitable and has a certainty of endless loss. Even its travelers agree on this truth, as do countless experts and people of insight and observation.

In conclusion, just like the other world's bliss, happiness in this world depends upon submitting to God and being His devoted servant. So always praise Him, saying: "Praise be to God for obedience and success in His way," and thank Him that we are Muslims.

The Fourth Word

The value of the Prescribed Prayers

In the Name of God, the All-Merciful, the All-Compassionate.

The Prescribed Prayers are the pillar of the Religion.

F YOU WISH TO FULLY UNDERSTAND THE IMPORTANCE AND VALUE OF the Prescribed Prayers, and with what little expense they are gained, and how crazy and at what great loss is the person who neglects them, consider the following parable: A ruler gives each of his two servants twenty-four gold coins and sends them to settle on one of his beautiful farms that is two months' travel away. He tells them: "Use this money to buy your ticket, your supplies, and what you will need after you arrive. After traveling for a day, you will reach a transit station. You can proceed from there either by car or by train or by ship or by plane. You can choose one according to your capital."

The servants leave. One spends only a little money before reaching the station. He uses his money so wisely that his master increases it a thousandfold. The other servant gambles away twenty-three of the twenty-four coins before reaching the station. The first servant advises the second one: "Use this coin to buy your ticket, or else you'll have to walk and suffer hunger. Our master is generous. Maybe he'll forgive you. Maybe you can take a plane, so we can reach the farm in a day. If not, you'll have to go on foot and endure two months of hunger and loneliness while crossing the desert." If he ignores his friend's advice, and instead of buying a ticket, which is like the key to a treasury, spends his remaining one coin on passing pleasures, anyone can understand how foolish and senseless he is.

Now, those of you who do not pray, as well as you, my soul that is not inclined toward the Prayer. The ruler is our Lord, our Creator. One servant represents religious people who pray with fervor; the other represents people who do not like to pray. The twenty-four coins are the twenty-four hours of a day. The farm is Paradise, the transit station is the grave, and the journey is human life from birth to the grave, and therefrom to eternal life. People cover the part of the journey from the grave to Paradise at different lengths of time according to their deeds and reverence for and obedience to God. Some of the truly devout pass in a day a thousand years like lightning, while others pass, like imagination, fifty thousand years. The Qur'an alludes to this truth in 22:47 and 70:4.[1]

The ticket is the Prescribed Prayers, all of which can be prayed in an hour. What a great loss one suffers who spends twenty-three hours a day on this brief worldly life and does not reserve the remaining hour for the Prescribed Prayers, and to what extent he wrongs himself; how unreasonably he behaves. Would not anyone who considers himself to be sensible understand how contrary to reason and wisdom and how far from sensibility it will be, if, considering it reasonable, one uses half of his money for a lottery being played by a thousand people and in which the possibility of winning is one in a thousand, but he does not spend one 24th of it on an eternal, inexhaustible treasure where the possibility of winning has been confirmed to be at ninety-nine out of a hundred?

Prayer comforts the soul, the heart, and the mind, and is not burdensome and trying for the body. Furthermore, if we regularly pray, correct, sincere intention transforms our daily, lawful deeds and conduct into worship. Thus our short lifetime is spent for the sake of eternal life in the other world, and our transient life gains some sort of permanence.

---

[1] ... A day with your Lord is like 1,000 years in your reckoning (32:5), and ... The angels and the spirit ascend to Him in a day, the measure of which is 50,000 years (of your normal worldly years) (70:4), respectively. (Tr.)

The Fifth Word

The right training for believers

In the Name of God, the All-Merciful, the All-Compassionate.

Surely God is with those Who refrain from disobeying Him in awe of Him and who do good deeds (as if they saw Him). (16:128)

F YOU WISH TO SEE WHAT A TRULY HUMAN DUTY AND WHAT A NATURAL, proper result of the creation of humanity it is to perform the Prescribed Prayers and avoid major sins, consider the following parable: During a war, two privates find themselves in a regiment, one well-trained and conscientious, and the other a recruit and a slave to his carnal soul. The well-trained, conscientous one attends training exercises and struggles against the enemy, without ever worrying about rations and allowances, because he knows it is the government's duty to supply the necessary military equipment, food, and when necessary, medical care. All he has to do is training for war and fighting for the country. However, he also helps out by supplying food and working in the kitchen. When asked what he is doing, he responds: "Some of the state's chores." He does not say he is working for his living. But the other soldier does not train or fight, for: "It's none of my business. It's a government matter." He cares only about his livelihood, and so deserts his regiment and goes to the marketplace to do shopping.

His well-trained friend advises him: "Brother, you're supposed to be training to fight for the country. That's why you're here. The government will meet your needs, because that's its duty. You can't meet all your needs regardless of time or place. As we're in a state of war, you might be accused of desertion or rebellion and be punished. There are two duties, one is the government's, and the others is ours. The government meets our needs, for which we also work to certain extent. Our duty is to prepare for fighting and to fight when necessary, with which the government helps us greatly." Imagine what trouble the second soldier will be in if he ignores his friend's words.

O my indolent soul! The turbulent battlefield represents our tumultous worldly life. The army divided into regiments represents humanity divided into nations. That particular regiment stands for the Muslim community in this century. One soldier is a devout and pious Muslim who knows what he is asked to do and so does the obligatory religious duties and avoids major sins, and struggles against his carnal, evil-commanding soul and Satan in order not to commit other sins. The other soldier is a sinful loser who is so obsessed with working for his livelihood as to accuse the true Bestower of provision, and so does not perform his religiously obligatory duties and commits many sins recklessly for the sake of earning his life. Training represents the duties of worship, including especially the Prescribed Prayers. The war stands for struggling against the carnal, evil-commanding soul and its lusts, and against the satans among the jinn and humanity, in order to be able to keep distant from sins and despicable morals, and to save the heart and spirit from eternal perdition. As for the duties: The first is giving life and maintaining it; while the other is worshipping and beseeching the One Who gives and maintains life, and trusting in Him.

Only He Who gives life, a most brilliant miracle of the Eternally Besought One's Art and a wonder of the Lord's Wisdom, sustains life with provision. Do you need convincing? The weakest and simplest animals are the best fed; like fish and worms in fruit. The least capable and most vulnerable creatures, such as babies or new-born animals, get the best food. It is enough to compare fish with foxes, the new-born with wild beasts, and trees with animals, in order to understand that the procurement of fundemantal, lawful food depends on neediness and impotence, rather than power and will.

So, those who ignore the Prescribed Prayers to pursue their livelihood are like the soldier who neglects his exercises, deserts the front for fear of hunger, and wanders around the marketplace. However, seeking one's rations from the kitchen of the All-Munificent Provider's Mercy after praying, and not burdening others is fine and proper. This too is a kind of worship.

Furthermore, our nature and spiritual being demonstrate that we are created to worship God. For in respect of our physical power and capability necessary for our worldly life, we cannot compete even with sparrows. But in respect of our knowledge necessary for our spiritual life and Hereafter, and of understanding our neediness, and supplication and worship, we are the king and commander of all animate creatures.

O my soul! If you consider this world your major goal and work for it, you will remain only a soldier with no more control over your affairs than a sparrow. But if you make the life of the Hereafter your aim, and make this life of the world the means of it and a field to be sown for it, and act accordingly, you will become the ruler of the animal kingdom, a beloved, supplicant servant of God Almighty, and His favored and honored guest in this world. You can choose either option. So ask for guidance and success on His way from the Most Merciful of the Merciful.

The Sixth Word

The supreme transaction

In the Name of God, the All-Merciful, the All-Compassionate.

God has bought from the believers their selves and their possessions in exchange for Paradise. (9:111)

F YOU WANT TO UNDERSTAND HOW PROFITABLE A TRANSACTION, how honorable a rank, it is to sell one's soul and property to God and to be His servant and soldier, listen to the following parable: Once a king entrusted two servants with one estate each, including all necessary workshops, machinery, horses, weapons, and other equipment. But as it was wartime, when everything is in flux, this merciful and compassionate king sent his noblest officer to them with the following message:

> Sell me the entrusted property so that I may keep it for you. Do not let it be destroyed in vain. After the war is over, I will return it to you in better shape than it was before. Furthermore, I will pay a great, higher price for it as if it was your own property. The machinery and tools will be used in my name at my workbench. Both the price and the fee for their use will be increased, maybe a thousandfold. I will give all the profit to you. You are weak and poor, and cannot pay for these great tasks. Let me take care of the expenses and equipment, and give you the income and profit. You can use it until demobilization. Consider these five advantages of this transaction.
>
> If you do not sell the property to me, consider this. As you see, no one is able to preserve what they possess. You too will lose what you now hold. It will go in vain, and you will miss out on the high price I offer you. All the delicate, precious tools and fine scales that are ready to be used will lose their value, since there are no metals worthy of their use. You will have to find some way to administer and preserve them. Moreover, you will be punished for betraying your trust. So consider the five ways you will lose.

By selling your property to me, you will become my soldier and act in my name. Far from being a mere recruit or irregular, you will be an honored and free officer of an exalted monarch.

After the two men had listened to this gracious decree, one said: "I'm honored and happy to sell. Thank you so much." The other was as proud, arrogant, selfish, and dissipated as Pharaoh. As if he would stay on that estate forever, he ignored the earthquakes and tumults and said: "No! Who is this king? I won't sell my property or diminish my comfort." After a while, the first man reached such a high rank that everyone envied his position. He had the king's favor and lived happily in the king's palace. The other one fell so low that everyone pitied him but realized that he deserved his position. As a result of his mistake, he forfeited his happiness and property, and suffered punishment and torment.

Now, O soul full of caprice, consider the truth displayed here. The king is the Monarch, Eternal before and after eternity, your Lord and Creator. That which He has entrusted to you represent your body, spirit, and heart, and so on, as well as your outer and inner senses such as sight, taste, intelligence, imagination. The noblest officer is the Messenger; the compassionate decree is the Qur'an, which states: *God has bought from the believers their selves and their possessions in exchange for Paradise* (9:111). The surging battlefield is the tempestuous surface of the world in flux, and causes everyone to reflect:

"Everything will leave our hands, perish, and be lost. Is there no way to make it eternal, to preserve it?" While engaged in such thoughts, the heavenly voice of the Qur'an is heard:

"There is a beautiful and easy way that offers five advantages or profits."

What is this way?

To sell the trust to its real Owner. The resulting five profits are:

FIRST PROFIT: The transient property becomes everlasting. This waning life, when given to the Eternal and Self-Subsistent Being of Majesty and spent for His sake, is transmuted into permanence and gives everlasting fruits. The moments of one's present life apparently vanish and rot, as do kernels and seeds. But then the flowers of happiness open and bloom in the Realm of Eternity, and each presents a luminous, lovely scene in the Intermediate Realm of the grave.

SECOND PROFIT: The price to be paid is Paradise.

THIRD PROFIT: The value of each bodily limb and sense is increased a thousandfold. For example, if you use your intelligence for the sake of your carnal soul, it becomes such an ill-omened, destructive, and debilitating instrument that it burdens you with sad sorrows of the past and terrifying fears of the future. This is why sinful people frequently resort to drunkenness or other frivolous pleasures. But if you sell your intelligence to its true Owner and use it on His behalf, it becomes like a mysterious key unlocking the infinite treasure-houses of compassion and wisdom-filled vaults, and elevates you to the rank of a pious and righteous guide deserving eternal happiness.

The eye is a window through which the spirit looks at this world. If you use it on behalf of your carnal soul, without selling it to God Almighty, by gazing at transient, impermanent beauties and spectacles, it panders to lust and other carnal desires. But if you sell it to its All-Seeing Maker and use it on His behalf and within His limits, it rises to the rank of a reader of the Great Book of the Universe,[2] a witness of the miracles of His creation, a blessed bee sucking on the blossoms of Mercy in the garden of this world.

Taste is another of the senses. If you do not sell it to your All-Wise Originator, but use it on behalf of your carnal soul and for the sake of your tongue or stomach, it sinks and declines to the level of a gatekeeper at the stomach's stable, a watchman at its factory. But if you sell it to the All-Munificent Provider, the sense of taste rises to the rank of a skilled overseer at Divine Compassion's treasure-houses, a grateful inspector in the kitchens of the Eternally Besought One's Power.

O intelligence, be careful! Think of what is an instrument of destruction and what is a key to all being. O eye! See the difference between an abominable panderer and a learned overseer of the Divine Library! O tongue! Taste well the difference between a stable doorkeeper or a factory watchman and the trustee of the treasure house of God's Mercy!

---

2 The universe, man and the Qur'an are three books which make the Creator known to us. The universe and man are created books which have issued from God's Attributes of Power and Will and are the collections of the manifestations of God's Names, while the Qur'an is their revealed counterpart. These three books interpret each other. Like the Qur'an, by studying the universe and man or himself, man acquires knowledge of God and draws close to Him. (Tr.)

When you compare all other instruments, faculties, and limbs to these, you understand that believers acquire a nature worthy of Paradise and unbelievers a nature conforming to Hell. Each attains its respective value. Due to their belief, believers use what the Creator has entrusted to them on His behalf and within His limits. Unbelievers betray the trust and use it for the sake of the carnal soul.

FOURTH PROFIT: Man is helpless but exposed to misfortune; he is indigent but has uncountable needs; and he is impotent, but the burden of life is very heavy. If he does not rely on the All-Powerful One of Majesty, trust in and submit to Him with full confidence, his conscience will always be troubled. He finds himself caught in vain torments, pains and regrets, all of which suffocate him. They either intoxicate him or turn him into a beast.

FIFTH PROFIT: Those who unveil the true nature of things and experience the truth agree that the reward for worshipping and glorifying God performed by your limbs, senses, and faculties will be given at the time of greatest need, in the form of Paradise's fruits.

If you refuse this transaction with its five-fold profit, in addition to being deprived of its profit, you suffer the following five-fold loss:

FIRST LOSS: Your beloved property and offspring, your adored carnal soul and its desires, and your foolishly loved youth and life all will vanish, burdening you with their sins and pains.

SECOND LOSS: You will be punished for betraying the trust, for you have wronged yourself by using the most precious tools on the most worthless objects.

THIRD LOSS: By debasing your precious faculties to a level much inferior to animals, you have insulted and transgressed against God's Wisdom.

FOURTH LOSS: In your helplessness and poverty, you will shoulder life's heavy burden and continually groan under the blows of transience and separation.

FIFTH LOSS: You convert the All-Merciful's fair gifts, such as the intellect, the heart, the eye, the tongue, meant to be used for laying the foundations of everlasting life and happiness in the Hereafter, into an ugly form, fit to open the gates of Hell before you.

We should make this bargain. Why do many people not want to make it? Is it so difficult? By no means! The resulting burdens are not hard. The limits of the religiously permissible enjoyment are broad and adequate for your desire, and so you do not need to indulge in what is forbidden. The duties imposed by God are light and few. To be His servant and soldier is an honor beyond description.

Your duty is to act and embark on all things in God's name, like a soldier, to receive and give on God's behalf, and to obey His permission and law. If you sin, seek His forgiveness by saying: "O Lord, forgive our sins and accept us as Your servants. Enable us to remain faithful to Your trust until the time of restitution arrives. Amin." And petition Him.

The Seventh Word

The door to human happinesss

In the Name of God, the All-Merciful, the All-Compassionate.

F YOU WANT TO UNDERSTAND HOW PRECIOUS A KEY TO REVEAL THE enigmatic riddle of the universe and open the door to happiness for the human spirit it is to belive in God and the Hereafter; and to understand how invaluable medicines for all ailments they are to patiently rely on your Creator and ask and pray to your Provider in gratitude, and seek refuge in Him; and also to understand how important, valuable and splendid a ticket for your journey to eternity, a light for the grave, and a provision for the next life they are to heed the Qur'an, abide by its laws, to perform the Prescribed Prayers, and to refrain from major sins[3]— if you want to understand all these, consider the following parable: Once a soldier in the middle of a battlefield and testing, in the arena of gain or loss, found himself in frightening circumstances. He was wounded on his right and left sides. Behind him was a lion ready to tear him apart, and ahead of him stood a gallows on which his friends and comrades were being hanged; it was awaiting him too. Before him lay a long road, which he had to travel. As the unfortunate soldier was pondering in despair, a wise, pious person appeared on his right and said: "Don't despair. I'll give you two talismans and teach you them. If you use them properly, the lion will become an obedient horse for you, and the gallows will become like a swing for your enjoyment. I'll also give you two medicines that will heal your wounds and make them smell like roses. Furthermore, I'll give you a ticket that allows

---

3 The major sins consist of associating partners with God; disrespecting one's parents; consuming the property of others, especially of orphans; engaging in usury; retreating when the army advances; slandering chaste women; committing crimes with a prescribed punishment (e.g., murder, adultery, fornication, theft); engaging in prohibited acts despite the Qur'an's or the Traditions' threat of a severe punishment for doing so in the next life; and deeds cursed by the Prophet. (Tr.)

you to travel the distance of years in one day. Try them and see if my words are true." The soldier did so a bit, and found his words true. I, this unfortunate Said, affirm it too. For I also tried them a bit and saw they were absolutely true.

Suddenly, a devilish, cunning man appeared on his left with ornate finery, pictures, fantasies and intoxicants, saying: "Hey, come on, friend! Let's enjoy ourselves, listen to music, look at these pictures of beautiful women, and eat and drink these delicious things." He asked the soldier what he was mumbling. The soldier replied: "A sacred invocation," to which the man said: "Leave these complicated issues. Let's not ruin our comfort. What's that in your hands?" The soldier replied: "Medicine." The man snorted: "Throw it away. There's nothing wrong with you. What's that paper with five seals upon it?" When the soldier said it was a ticket and a rations card, the man said: "Tear them up! How can you think of going anywhere on such a beautiful spring day?" This is how that devilish man tried to lead the soldier astray. The soldier eventually has been tempted a bit to follow, for he is human and thus subject to deception.

To his right, the soldier suddenly hears a thunder-like voice: "Wake up! Don't be deceived. Say to that devil: 'If you can kill the lion, do so. If you can remove the gallows, do so. If you can heal my wounds, do so. If you can arrange it so that I will not travel this road before me, do so. Do these things, and then we can enjoy ourselves. If you cannot, be quiet!'"

Thus, O my soul, which laughed in its youth and now weeps at its laughter! The soldier represents you and every other human being. The lion is our appointed hour of death, while the gallows stand for our continual separation from friends. The two wounds are our infinite and troublesome impotence and our grievous and boundless poverty. The travel is the long journey of testing passing through the World of Spirits, our life as an embryo, our youth, old age, the grave, the Place of Resurrection and Supreme Gathering, and the Sirat (the "Bridge" which leads to Hell or Heaven). The two talismans are belief in God and the Hereafter.

Understand: *Belief in God and the Hereafter*. Through this sacred talisman death (the lion) becomes like an obedient horse to take believers from the dungeon of the world to the gardens of Paradise, to the presence of the All-Merciful One. It is because of this that the pious and learned, those who have a true understanding of death, are not afraid of dying and actually wish to die even before their appointed time. The passage of time, punctuated by separation from friends (because of death, represented by gallows), is transformed by belief into a means to watch with perfect pleasure the perpetually renewed and always colorful embroideries of God's wonderful acts, His Power's miracles, and His Compassion's manifestations. Its like is this: Since the "mirrors" reflecting the colors in the sunlight and the scenes of a film are varied and replaced, the resulting views are even more beautiful.

As for the medicines: one is patience and trusting in God, relying on His Power, and having confidence in His Wisdom. What is there to fear when, realizing our helplessness, we rely upon the Owner of the command, *Be, and it is* (36:82)[4]? Even when confronted with a most frightening situation and a great calamity, he says: *Surely, to God do we belong, and to Him is our return* (2:156), and places his trust in his All-Compassionate Lord with utmost serenity. Those who have true knowledge of God are content to realize their helplessness before God and put their hope in His judgment. There is pleasure in the fear of God. If a one-year old were asked what is the most pleasant thing he or she knows, the reply would be: "Taking refuge in my mother's warm embrace, conscious of my weakness and helplessness—from her sweetest slap." As a mother's compassion is only a small spark from God's Compassion, people of perfection take great pleasure in their helplessness and fear of God. Forsaking what is in their power, they take refuge in God and make their fear and helplessness a means of intercession before Him.

The other medicine is petitioning God with thanksgiving and contentment, and relying upon the Munificent All-Provider's mercy. How could the guests of an All-Munificent Provider, Who has made the earth's surface as a table and the spring for flowers to put on that table, regard their own poverty and helplessness before God as unbearable? Their poverty and need become their appetite, and so they try to increase their poverty. This is why spiritually perfect people are proud of their poverty. However, do not misunderstand this! It means to be aware of one's poverty before God and to entreat Him, not to parade poverty before the people and assume the air of a beggar.

The ticket to eternity comprises the Prescribed Prayers, observing the other obligations, and avoiding the major sins. All people of discernment and learning agree that the only way to get a light, some provisions, and

---

[4] *When He wills a thing to be, He but says to it "Be!" and it is.* (36:82). (Tr.)

a vehicle for the long journey to eternity is to abide by the Qur'an's commands and prohibitions. Science, philosophy, and craftsmanship alone are not worth much, for they only light the road as far as the grave.

O my indolent soul! How easy and light it is to perform the five daily Prayers and renouncing the seven major sins, and how important and great their results are. If you understand the truth here, you will say to the devilish one who tries to seduce you into vice and dissipation: "If you have the means to abolish death, impotence, and poverty, and close the door on the grave, then tell us and let's heed it. Otherwise, be still! In the greatest mosque of the universe, the Qur'an reads the universe, so let's listen to it. Let's become filled with its light and act according to its guidance. Let's read it regularly! It is its right to speak and what it says is true. The Qur'an is the truth, coming from the Ultimate Truth. It guides to the truth, spreading its light everywhere."

> O God, illuminate our hearts with the light of belief and the Qur'an. Enrich us with the perception and offering of our poverty before You. Don't impoverish us with indifference toward You. We have given up our power and strength for Your sake and taken refuge in Your Power and Might, so make us among those who place their trust in You. Do not leave us to ourselves. Preserve us with Your preserving. Have mercy on us and all believing men and women.
>
> Bestow blessings and peace upon our master Muhammad, Your servant and Prophet, Your chosen one and intimate friend—the beauty of Your Kingdom, the foremost of Your creation, the focus of Your affection, and the sun of Your guidance; the tongue of Your proofs, the embodiment of Your Mercy, the light of Your creation, and the glory of Your creatures; the lamp of Your Oneness among the multiplicity of Your creatures; the discloser of the mystery of Your creation; the herald of Your Lordship's Kingdom; the preacher of what pleases You; the proclaimer of Your Names' Treasures; the teacher of Your servants; the interpreter of Your signs; the mirror of Your Lordship's Beauty; the means of witnessing You and bearing witness to You; Your beloved one and Messenger whom You sent as a mercy to the worlds—and upon his Family and Companions, his fellow Prophets and Messengers, Your angels brought near to You, and Your righteous servants. Amin.

The Eighth Word

The necessity of religion

In the Name of God, the All-Merciful, the All-Compassionate.

God, there is no deity but He, the All-Living, the Self-Subsisting (by Whom all subsist). (2:255)

The religion with God is Islam. (3:19)

F YOU WANT TO PERCEIVE THE TRUE NATURE OF THE WORLD AND human spirit within it, and the religion's nature and its value for humanity; if you want to perceive how the absence of the True Religion makes this world the darkest dungeon and the unbeliever the most unfortunate creature, and why belief in God's Existence and Unity, as well as reliance upon Him, opens the universe's secret sign and saves our souls from darkness—if you want to perceive all these, consider the following parable:

Two brothers travel together. Coming to a fork in the road, they see a wise old man and ask him which way to take. He tells them: "The way to the right requires observance of certain laws but this observance brings a certain security and happiness, while the road to the left promises a certain kind of freedom but within this freedom lie certain danger and distress. Now, the choice is yours!"

The well-disciplined, well-mannered brother, relying on God, takes the right way and accepts dependence on law and order.

The other brother, who is immoral and a layabout, takes the left way for the sake of freedom. He seems comfortable, but in fact feels no inner tranquillity. Reaching a desert, he suddenly hears the terrible sound of a beast that is about to attack him. He runs away and, seeing a waterless well 60 meters deep, jumps into it. Halfway down, he grabs a tree growing out of the wall to break his fall. The tree has two roots, both of which are being gnawed away by two rats, one white and the other black. Looking up, he sees the beast waiting for him. Looking down, he sees a horrible dragon almost at his feet, its large mouth open to receive him. Looking at the wall, he notices that it is covered with laboring insects. Looking again at the tree, he notices that although it is only a fig tree, it miraculously has many different fruits growing on it, such as walnuts and pomegranates.

Hanging in the well, he does not understand all that has happened. Unable to reason, he cannot imagine that all of these things are not there by chance, and that they must have some significant meaning. He cannot grasp that there must be one who causes all these things to happen that way. Although inwardly distressed, and despite his spirit's and heart's complaints, his carnal, evil-commanding soul pretends everything is fine and so ignores their weeping. Pretending that he is enjoying himself in a garden, he starts eating all kinds of fruits—for free. But some of them are poisonous and will harm him.

In a *hadith qudsi*,[5] God says: "I will treat My servants in the way they think of Me."[6] This man sees everything happening to him as having no meaning, and thus that is the way it is for him. So he is and will be treated in the way he thinks and sees. He neither dies nor lives well, but merely persists in an agony of suspense.

Recalling the other, well-disciplined, wise brother, let us see his situatuion. Since he is well-mannered and has a good character, he always thinks of the good, affirms and observes the law, and feels secure and free. Finding beautiful flowers and fruits together with certain ruined and ugly things in a garden, he focuses on what is good and beautiful. His brother cannot, for he has concerned himself with what is ruined and ugly and finds no ease in such a garden. The wise brother lives according to: "Look on the good side of everything," and so is generally happy with everything.

On his way he too reaches a desert, just as his brother did, and a beast shows up. He too is afraid but not as much as his brother, because he contemplates that there must be an owner and ruler of the desert and that the beast must be in his service and under his command. He also jumps down a well and, halfway down, catches hold of some tree branches. Noticing two

---

[5] *Hadith Qudsi*: This is a specific category of sayings from the Prophet. The wording is the Prophet's, but the meaning belongs to God directly. (Tr.)

[6] *Sahih al-Bukhari*, "Tawhid" 15, 35; *Sahih Muslim*, "Dhikr" 2, 19, *Sunan at-Tirmidhi*, "Zuhd" 51.

rats gnawing at the tree's two roots, as well as the dragon below and the beast above, he finds himself in a strange situation. But unlike his brother, since he has a good character, which causes him to think positively and see the good side of everything, he infers that everything must have been arranged by someone and constitute a sign. Thinking that he is being watched and examined, he understands that he is being directed and guided as a test and for a purpose. His curiosity aroused, he asks: "Who wants to make me know him and guides me to a certain point along such a strange way?" This curiosity arouses in him a love for the sign's owner, which makes him want to understand the sign, what the events mean, and to acquire good qualities to please its owner.

He realizes that the tree is a fig tree, although it bears many kinds of fruit. He is no longer afraid, for he realizes that it is a sample catalogue of the unseen owner's fruits that he has prepared in his garden for his guests. Otherwise, one tree would not bear so many different fruits. He starts to pray earnestly and, as a result, the key to the secret is inspired in him. He declares: "O owner of this scene and events, I am in your hands. I take refuge in you and am at your service. I desire your approval and knowledge of you." The wall opens, revealing a door (the dragon's mouth) leading onto a wonderful, pleasant garden. Both the dragon and the beast become two servants inviting him in. The beast changes into a horse on which he rides.

And so, my lazy soul and imaginary friend! Let's compare their positions and see how good brings good and evil brings evil. The brother who took the left way of self-trust and self-willed freedom is about to fall into the dragon's mouth, trembling with fear. He is always anxious, lonely, and in despair, and considers himself a prisoner facing the attacks of wild beasts. He adds to his distress by eating apparently delicious but actually poisonous fruits that are only samples; they are not meant to be eaten for their own sake, but to persuade people to seek the originals and become customers of them. He changes his day into darkness. He wrongs himself, changing his situation into a hell-like one, so that he neither deserves pity nor has the right to complain.

In contrast, the brother who took the right way is in a fruitful garden and surrounded by servants. He studies every different and beautiful incident in awe, with a pleasant fear, and a lovely quest for knowledge. In hope and with yearning, he sees himself as an honored guest enjoying himself with his generous host's strange and beautiful servants. He does not eat up the fig tree's fruits; rather, he samples them and, understanding reality, postpones his pleasure and enjoys the anticipation.

The first brother is like one who denies his favored situation at a banquet in a summer garden surrounded by friends, and instead, becoming drunk, imagines himself among wild beasts in winter and complains thereof. Wronging himself and insulting his friends, he deserves no mercy. The other brother, who accepts trustingly what is given and observes the law, sees and accepts reality, which for him is beautiful. Having perceived the beauty of the reality, he respects the perfection of the owner of the reality, and therefore deserves his mercy. Thus can we attain a partial understanding of: *Whatever good befalls you is from God, and whatever ill befalls you is from yourself* (4:79).

Reflecting upon the brothers, we see that one's carnal, evil-commanding soul prepared a hell-like situation for him, corresponding to his own attitude of reality, whereas the other's potential goodness, positive intention, and good nature led him to a very favored and happy situation. Now, I say to my own soul as well as to the one who is listening to this story together with my soul: If you want to be the fortunate brother in the parable, not the unfortunate one, listen to the Qur'an, obey its decrees, follow its guidance.

The gist of the parable is as follows: One brother is a believing spirit, a righteous heart; the other is an unbelieving spirit, a vice, transgressing heart. The right way is that of the Qur'an and belief; the left way is that of unbelief and rebellion. The garden is the transient human social life, which has both good and evil, clean and polluted aspects. A sensible person "takes what is clear and pleasant, leaves what is turbid and distressing," and proceeds with a tranquil heart. The desert is the earth, the beast is death, the well is our life, and 60 meters is our average lifespan of 60 years.

The tree in the well is life, the two rats gnawing on its roots are day and night, and the dragon is the grave's opening. For a believer, it is no more than a door opening onto the Garden. The insects are the troubles we face, and in reality are God's gentle warnings that prevent believers from becoming heedless. The fruits are the bounties of this world presented as samples from the blessings of the Hereafter, inviting customers toward the fruits of Paradise. The tree with various fruits shows the unique stamp of Divine Power, the peculiar seal of Divine Lordship, and the inimitable signature of the Divine Sovereignty, Whose unique virtue is "to create everything out of one thing" and "to change everything into one thing"; to make various plants and fruits from the same soil; to create all living things from one drop of water; and to nourish and sustain all living things in the same manner but through different foods. Creating everything out of one thing and changing everything into one thing is a sign, a mark, peculiar to the Creator of everything, Who has power over everything. The sign shows the secret will of God in creating. It is opened with belief, and its key is: "O God, there is no deity but God; God, there is no deity but He, the All-Living, the Self-Subsisting."

For one brother, for the people of the Qur'an and belief, the dragon's mouth (the grave) changes into a door opening onto the gardens of eternity in Paradise from the dungeon of the world and the arena of testing, onto the mercy of the All-Merciful from the troubles of the worldly life. For the other, as for all people of misguidance and rebellion, it is the door to a narrow, suffocating place of torment. The beast changing into an obedient servant, a disciplined and trained horse means that for unbelievers death is a painful separation from loved ones, an imprisonment after leaving their deceiving, worldly paradise. For believers, it is a means of reunion with dead friends and companions. It is like going to their eternal home of happiness, a formal invitation to pass into the eternal gardens, an occasion to receive the wage to be bestowed by the All-Compassionate and Merciful One's generosity for services rendered to Him, and a kind of retirement from the burden of life.

In sum, those who pursue this transient life place themselves in hell, even though they stay in what appears—to them—as a paradise on the earth. Those who seek the eternal life find peace and happiness in both worlds. Despite all troubles they may suffer in the world, they show patience and thank God, as they see the world as the waiting room for Paradise.

> O God, make us among the people of happiness, salvation, the Qur'an, and belief! Amin. O God, bestow peace and blessings upon our master Muhammad, and upon his Family and Companions, to the number of all letters contained in the Qur'an, reflected by the permission of the All-Merciful in the sound waves of each word recited by Qur'anic reciters from its first revelation to the end of time. Have mercy on us and our parents, and on all believers to the number of those words, through Your Mercy, O Most Merciful of the Merciful. Amin. All praise and gratitude are for God, the Lord of all the worlds.

The Twelfth Word

A brief comparison between the Qur'an's wisdom and human philosophy and scientism

In the Name of God, the All-Merciful, the All-Compassionate.

Whoever has been given the Wisdom, certainly has been given much good. (2:269)

[NOTE: The two Fundamentals chosen out of the Four Fundamentals in this Word present a brief comparison between the Qur'an's sacred wisdom and human philosophy, and a concise summary of the Qur'anic instruction and training for humanity's personal and social life.]

The Second Fundamental

COMPARISON BETWEEN THE QUR'AN'S MORAL TRAINING IN ONE'S personal life and that of philosophy: A sincere student of philosophy is a Pharaoh-like tyrant;[7] he is a contemptible tyrant who bows in adoration before the meanest thing, if he perceives it to be in his interest. That irreligious student is obstinate and refractory; but he is so wretched that he accepts endless degradation for one pleasure. He is unbending but so mean as to kiss the feet of devilish people for a base advantage. He is also conceited and domineering, but, unable to find any point of support in his heart, he is an utterly impotent and vainglorious tyrant. That student is a self-centered egoist who only strives to gratify his material and carnal desires; a sneaky egotist who pursues the realization of his personal interests in certain national interests.

---

[7] Pharaoh is a title given to the kings of ancient Egypt, and signifies any tyrant one. (Tr.)

However, a sincere student of the Qur'an is a worshipping servant of God, but he does not degrade himself by bowing in worship before even the greatest of the created. He is a dignified servant who does not take even a supreme benefit like Paradise as the aim of his worship. He is modest, mild and gentle, yet he does not lower himself voluntarily before anybody other than his Originator, unless He allows him to do so. He is also aware of his innate weakness and need, but he is independent due to the other-worldly wealth that his Munificent Owner has stored up in him; and he is powerful because he relies on his Master's infinite Power. He acts and strives purely for God's sake and good pleasure, and to be equipped with virtue. The training given by the Qur'an and philosophy may be understood through the above comparison.

The Third Fundamental

The Moral training of the Qur'an and philosophy in human social life: Philosophy considers force or might to be the point of support in social life, and the realization of self-interest is its goal. It holds that the principle of life is conflict. The unifying bonds between the members of a community and communities are race and aggressive nationalism; and the fruits philosophy offers are the gratification of carnal desires and the continuous increase of human needs. However, force calls for aggression, seeking self-interest causes fighting over material resources, and conflict brings strife. Racism feeds by swallowing others, thereby paving the way for aggression. This is why humanity has lost happiness.

As for the Qur'anic wisdom, it accepts right, not might, as the point of support in social life. Its goal is virtue and God's approval, not the realization of self-interests. Its principle of life is mutual assistance, not conflict. The only community bonds it accepts are those of religion, profession, and country. Its final aims are controlling carnal desires and urging the soul to sublime matters, satisfying our exalted feelings so that we will strive for human perfection and true humanity. Right calls for unity, virtues bring solidarity, and mutual assistance means hastening to help one another. Religion secures brotherhood, sisterhood, and cohesion. Restraining our carnal soul and desires and urging the soul to perfection brings happiness in this world and the next.

The Thirteenth Word

Conversations with young people and prisoners

In the Name of God, the All-Merciful, the All-Compassionate.

[NOTE: A conversation held with young people surrounded by temptation but still able to judge what is happening around them.]

 OME YOUNG PEOPLE, SEEKING TO COUNTER MODERN AMUSEMENTS and fancies and so save themselves from punishment in the Hereafter, sought help from the *Risale-i Nur*. In its name, I told them what follows:

The grave is there, no one can deny it. Whether they want or not, everyone will enter it. It is represented in three ways, there is not the forth:

For believers, it is the door to a more beautiful world. For those who admit the next life but live a misguided, dissipated life, it is the door to solitary imprisonment that will separate them from their loved ones. Since they believe and confirm but do not live according to their belief, that is exactly how they will be punished. For unbelievers and the misguided who do not believe in the Hereafter, it is the door to eternal execution. Since they believe death to be an execution without resurrection, they will be punished eternally.

Death may come at any time without differentiating between young and old; its appointed hour is unknown. Such an awesomely threatening reality makes it our greatest, most urgent matter to search for a way to avoid eternal punishment and imprisonment, for a way to change the grave into a door opening onto a permanent world of light and eternal happiness.

Death will be experienced in these three ways, as has been reported by 124,000 truthful reporters—the Prophets, in whose hands are signs of truthfulness (miracles). Their reports have been confirmed by millions of saints relying on their discernment, vision, and intuition. Also, innumerable truth-seeking scholars have proved it rationally with their decisive proofs at the level of "certainty based on knowledge." All groups agree that only belief in and obedience to God can save one from eternal punishment and imprisonment, and make the grave a way to eternal happiness.

If only one reliable reporter warns that a particular way carries a one percent risk of death, people will be so afraid that they will avoid it. But countless truthful, authoritative reporters—Prophets, saints, and truth-seeking scholars—have provided proof of their truth and warn us that misguidance and dissipation carry a hundred percent risk of death followed by eternal punishment. In contrast, belief and worship change the grave into a door opening onto an eternal treasury, a palace of lasting happiness. If we, especially those of us claiming to be Muslims, do not truly believe and worship in the face of such a mighty warning, how will we overcome our anxieties while waiting to die, even if we were given the rule of the whole world and enjoyed all its pleasures?

Seeing old age, illness, misfortune, and numerous instances of death everywhere reopens our pain and reminds us of death. Even if the misguided and the dissolute appear to enjoy all kinds of pleasure and delight, they most certainly are in a hellish state of spiritual torment. However, a profound stupor of heedlessness makes them temporarily insensible to it.

Obedient believers experience the grave as the door to an eternal treasury and endless happiness. Since the "belief coupon" they have causes them to have a priceless ticket from the allocations of eternal Divine Destiny, they expect the call "come and collect your ticket" with profound pleasure and spiritual delight. If this pleasure could assume the material form of a seed, it would grow into a private paradise. But those who abandon this great delight and pleasure to indulge the drives of youth, who choose temporary and illicit pleasures, which resemble poisonous honey causing limitless pains, fall far below the status of animals.

They are not like Western unbelievers, who may recognize another Prophet even if they deny their own; who may yet recognize God even if they deny all Prophets; or who may have some good qualities, which are means to certain perfections, even if they do not recognize God. Muslims, however, know the Prophets, God, and all perfections because of Prophet Muhammad, upon him be peace and blessings, and so those Muslims who abandon the Prophet's instruction and break with his line cannot recognize any other Prophet or find support in their souls to preserve any human perfection. For Prophet Muhammad is the last and greatest Prophet; superior to all with respect to his mission, miracles, and accomplishments; and came with a universal religion and Message for all time and peoples. Muslims who abandon this Pride of humankind's principles of training and the rules of his religion will most certainly be unable to find any light or achieve any perfection. They will be condemned to absolute loss and decline.

So, those of you who are addicted to worldly pleasure, and in anxiety at the future, struggle to secure it and your lives, if you want pleasure and delight, happiness and ease in this world, be content with what is religiously lawful. It is sufficient for your enjoyment. You must have understood by now that each forbidden pleasure contains many pains. If the dissolute were shown their future—their states in fifty years from now—in the way past events are shown in the movie theater, they would be horrified and disgusted with themselves. Those who wish to be eternally happy in both worlds should follow the Prophet's instruction on the firm ground of belief.

A warning and lesson to a group of unhappy young people

One day several bright young people came to me. They were seeking an effective deterrent to the dangers arising from modern worldly life, youth, and animal desires. I spoke to them as I had spoken to a group of young people who had previously sought help from the *Risale-i Nur*:

Your youth will definitely disappear. If you do not remain within the bounds of what is religiously lawful, it will be lost and, rather than pleasure, it will bring you suffering and calamities here, in the grave, and in the Hereafter. But if you adhere to Islamic discipline and spend it chastely, uprightly and in worship in gratitude to the blessings of youth, in effect, your youth will remain perpetually and be the cause of gaining eternal youth.

A life without belief, or with belief rendered ineffective by rebelliousness, only produces pain, sorrow, and grief that far exceed the superficial, fleeting enjoyment and resulting pleasure. This is because humanity has intelligence and, unlike animals, is connected to the past, present, and future, and derives both pain and pleasure from them. Whereas animals have no intelligence and therefore neither sorrows to arise from the past nor fears and anxieties concerning the future spoil their present pleasure. But such sorrows and anxieties plague the misguided and heedless, marring their pleasure and diluting it with pain. If this pleasure is illicit, it becomes like poisonous honey.

Given this, we are far lower than animals when it comes to life's enjoyments. In fact, the lives of misguided, heedless people consists only of the day in which they find themselves, as is the case with their entire existence and world. According to their misguided belief, that which is past no longer exists. But their intellect, which connects them to the past and the future, produces only darkness, and their lack of belief in eternal life makes the future non-existent for them. It is this non-existence that makes separations eternal and continually darkens their lives. In contrast, a life built upon belief results in the past and the future being illuminated and acquiring existence through the light of belief. Such a life also provides exalted spiritual pleasures and lights of existence for their spirits and hearts.

This is the reality of life. If you want to enjoy life, animate it with belief, adorn it with religious obligations, and maintain it by avoiding sins.

As for the fearsome reality of death, which is demonstrated by deaths everywhere and always, the following parable will suffice: Imagine that we are facing a gallows. Beside it is a lottery office selling tickets for truly high prizes. Each of us, willingly or not, will be invited there. Since our appointed hour is unknown, they will call us any time, saying: "Come to the gallows for execution!" or "You have won a huge prize! Come and collect it!"

While we are waiting, a woman and a man approach us. The woman is scantily clad, beautiful, and alluring. She holds in her hand some apparently very delicious, but in fact poisonous, sweets and offers them to us. The man, who is honest and solemn, comes up behind her and says: "I have brought you a talisman, a lesson. If you study it and don't eat the sweets, you will be saved from the gallows, and you will receive the winning ticket with this talisman. You see that those who eat the sweets inevitably mount the gallows, and further, they suffer dreadful stomach pains from the poison of the sweets until they mount them. Those who receive the ticket also mount the gallows, but millions of witnesses testify that instead of being hanged, they use the gallows as a step to enter the prize arena easily. So, look from the windows! The highest officials, the high-ranking persons connected with this business, proclaim: "Just as you see clearly those people mounting the gallows, so be certain that those who have the talisman will receive the ticket for the prize."

Thus, the dissolute, religiously forbidden pleasures of youth are like poisonous sweets. Since they cause people to lose their belief, their ticket to an eternal treasury and a document for everlasting happiness, those who follow them are subject to be hanged on the gallows and suffer the tribulations of the grave, which is the door to eternal darkness for them. As the hour of death is unknown, the executioner may come at any time without differentiating between young and old. But if you abandon religiously forbidden pleasures and acquire the Qur'anic talisman (belief and performing religious obligations), 124,000 Prophets and innumerable saints unanimously inform us that you will receive the ticket for the treasury of eternal happiness from the extraordinary lottery of Destiny. They also show its signs and proofs.

In short, youth passes. Wasting it results in infinite misfortune and pain in both worlds. If you want to understand how many of such youths end up in hospitals with mental and physical diseases, mainly because of their abuse, in prisons or hostels for the destitute due to their excesses, and in bars because of the distress provoked by their spiritual unease, go and ask at those places. As you will hear from the mute eloquence of hospitals' tongue the moans and groans of those who pursued youth's appetites, so will you hear from prisons the regretful sighs of unhappy people imprisoned mainly for illicit actions due to their "youthful excesses." You will also understand that most torments of the grave are due to a misspent youth, as related by saints who can discern the life of the grave (the Intermediate Realm), and affirmed by all scholars of truth.

Further, consult the elderly and the sick. Most of them will answer you with grief and regret: "Alas! We wasted our youths in frivolity. Be careful not to do as we did!" Those who do not control the illicit passions of five to ten years' youth bring upon themselves grief and sorrow in this world, torment and harm in the Intermediate Realm, and the severe punishment of Hell in the Hereafter. Although they might be in a most pitiable situation, since they freely chose to pursue such a path, they are not worthy of pity. For one who is freely resigned to harm is not worthy of pity. May Almighty God save all of us from the alluring temptations of this age and preserve us against them. Amin.

A conversation with prisoners

In His Name, All-Glorified is He.

Prisoners are in great need of the *Risale-i Nur*'s consolation; especially those who suffered the blow of youth and spend the prime of their lives in prison need the Risale-i Nur as much as they need bread. Youths are driven by emotion rather than reason. Emotion and desire are blind; they cannot see consequences and prefer an ounce of immediate pleasure to tons of future pleasure. They kill for a minute's satisfaction of revenge, and then suffer uncountable hours of painful imprisonment. One hour of dissolute pleasure spent in committing rape may destroy a lifetime's contentment through the fear of prison and enemies.

Young people meet many pitfalls that cause them to transform life's sweetness into a most bitter and remorse-laden existence. In particular, a huge and mighty state to the north is misusing its youths' passions and shaking this century with its storms. For it has made lawful for its blind-emotion driven young people the beautiful daughters and wives of upright, innocent people. By allowing men and women to go together to public baths, it encourages immorality. It also allows the vagabond and the poor to use freely, even plunder, the property of the rich. Everyone trembles in the face of this calamity.

During this age, Muslim youths must act heroically and respond to this two-pronged attack with "sharp swords" like the *Risale-i Nur*'s "Fruits (of Belief)" and "A Guide for Youth." Otherwise, those unfortunate youths will destroy their future, their happiness in both worlds, their eternal afterlife, and transform both into suffering. They will wind up in hospitals due to their abused energy and dissipation, in prisons due to their excesses, and be full of regret when they are old. But if they protect themselves with Qur'anic training and the Islamic truths, some of which the *Risale-i Nur* expounds, they will become truly heroic youths, perfect human beings, prosperous Muslims, and in some ways masters over the rest of animate beings.

If young people in prisons spend just one hour a day on the five Prescribed Prayers, and while imprisonment prevents the perpetration of many sins, avoid other painful sins and seek God's forgiveness for the crime that led them to their present state, both their own future and their relatives, nation, and country will benefit. In addition, the Qur'an of miraculous exposition and all other revealed Scriptures give the certain, glad tidings that their fleeting ten to fifteen years of youth will gain them an eternal, brilliant youth. If young people act in gratitude for the delightful blessing of youth by following the Straight Path in obedience to God, the blessing increases and becomes eternal and even more pleasurable. If they do not, they are pursued by calamity, pain, and grief. Their lives become nightmarish and then disappear. They live aimlessly, and so harm both their relatives and their nation and country.

If those who have been imprisoned unjustly perform the Prescribed Prayers will find that each hour spent behind bars equals one day of worship. Their cells will become like a place of retreat for them, and they themselves may be considered among the pious people of old times who retreated to caves to devote themselves to worship. If they are poor or aged or ill and seek to learn the truths of belief, will find that each hour spent in prison will equal twenty hours of worship, provided they seek God's forgiveness for the crime they committed and perform the religious obligations. The prison will resemble a rest house, a place of friendliness owing to those who compassionately care after them, and a place of training, and education. Staying in prison may even bring them greater happiness than they could find on the outside, for there they would be perplexed and assaulted by sin. If they receive proper education while in prison, former murderers or revenge-seekers would be released as repentant, mature, and well-behaved people who can benefit their nation. Those who saw the Denizli prisoners attain this rank quickly through the moral instruction of the Risale-i Nur remarked: If, instead of fifteen years of imprisonment, they receive a fifteen-week instruction from the *Risale-i Nur*, this will reform them much better.

Since death does not die and the appointed hour is unknown, it may come at any time; since the grave cannot be closed, and people enter it in successive convoys; and since the Qur'an declares that believers experience death as a discharge from worldly duties and that belief saves them from eternal punishment, while unbelievers experience death as an execution leading to everlasting torment and unending separation from their loved ones and all other creatures, for sure, the happiest people are those who thank God in patience and, benefiting from their time in prison, take the necessary moral and religious teaching to serve the Qur'an and belief on the Straight Path.

O addicts of enjoyment and pleasure! I am now seventy-five years old. I have come to know with utmost certainty from thousands of experiences and proofs that true enjoyment, pure pleasure, grief-free joy, and happiness are found only in belief and the sphere of its truths. One worldly pleasure yields many pains, as if delivering ten slaps for a single grape, and thus mars the pleasure of life.

O you unfortunate people suffering imprisonment! Since you are mourning here and your life is bitter, benefit from your time in prison so that you may not mourn in the Hereafter and so that your eternal life may be sweet. Just as an hour's watch under severe battle conditions sometimes equals a year of worship, the hardship of each hour spent worshipping in prison multiplies and changes hardship into mercy.

An effective solace for prisoners

In His Name, All-Glorified is He.
Upon you be peace and God's mercy and blessing!

My dear, truthful brothers!

I will offer an effective solace for prisoners and for those who kindly help them and supervise their food, which comes from outside.

FIRST POINT: Each day spent in prison may gain as much reward as ten days of worship, and with regard to their fruits, may transform these transient hours into enduring hours, and a few years of punishment may be the means of salvation from millions of years of eternal imprisonment. Imprisoned believers can gain this most significant and valuable advantage by praying five times a day, by asking God's forgiveness for the sins that led to their imprisonment, and by thanking God patiently. Prison is an obstacle to certain sins; it prevents them.

SECOND POINT: Just as the disappearance of pleasure brings pain, the disappearance of pain brings pleasure. When thinking of past happy and enjoyable days, everyone feels regret and longing and utters a sigh of grief. When recalling past calamitous and painful days, everyone feels pleasure because they are gone, thanks God that such days are past and have left their reward, and sighs with relief. This means, an hour's temporary pain leaves an immaterial pleasure in the spirit, while an hour's pleasure leaves pain.

Such is reality. Past hours of misfortune and their pain have disappeared, while the future days of imagined distress have not yet come. Pain does not come from nothing or from that which does not exist. Therefore, it is pure lunacy to eat and drink continually today out of fear that we will probably be hungry and thirsty in the future. Similarly, it is foolish to think at this present moment of past and future pains—pains which do not exist—and, as a result, to grow impatient, to ignore one's faulty soul, and to act as though one is complaining about God. If we do not waste our precious stores of patience on worrying about the past and the future, neither of which exists, it will cause our existing pain to decrease tenfold.

This is not a complaint: During this third period of my stay in the "School of Joseph," a few days of physical and spiritual affliction and illness, which stem mainly from the despair I felt at not being able to serve the Qur'an and the like of which I had never before experienced, began to crush me. However, after Divine grace showed me this truth, I accepted my distressing illness and imprisonment. Since it is of great profit for a poor man like me, who waits at the door of the grave, to turn an hour of possible heedlessness into ten hours of worship, I thanked God.

THIRD POINT: There is a great reward to be had from attending compassionately to the needs of prisoners, from providing their food and soothing their spiritual wounds. Serving them the food which is sent from outside also brings the same spiritual reward as one would gain if that food were to be given away as alms. This reward is added to the records of good deeds of both the prison guards and those who contribute to it from within and outside the prison. If the prisoners are old, sick, poor, or without support or protection, the reward of such alms-giving multiplies. To gain this valuable profit, however, one must perform the daily canonical Prayers so that their service may be only for God's sake. In addition, one should hasten to help prisoners with sincerity, compassion, and cheerfulness, and in such a manner that they do not feel themselves placed under obligation to you.

Advice to prisoners

In His Name, All-Glorified is He.

There is not a thing but it glorifies Him with praise.

Upon you be peace and His mercy and blessing everlastingly!

My friends in prison and brothers and sisters in religion!

I will explain a truth that will save you from torment here and in the Hereafter. Imagine that someone killed your sibling or relative. One minute of satisfaction derived from revenge will cause uncountable minutes of distress and imprisonment, and the fear of retaliation and the anxiety of always being pursued will drive all pleasure and enjoyment out of life. Thus you will suffer both fear and vexation. The only solution is the reconciliation encouraged by the Qur'an and by truth, humanity, and being a Muslim as well.

Right, truth, and mutual advantage require reconciliation. As each one's death comes at its fixed time, the victim would not have lived any longer anyway. God's decree was executed via the murderer. Unless they are reconciled, both parties will continue to suffer from fear and vindictiveness. This is why Islam says that a believer should not be angry or hold a grudge against another believer for more than three days.

If the murder was not the result of a grudge or enmity, and a hypocritical one instigated it, the parties must make peace without delay so that this minor disaster will not grow and persist. If they do so, and the murderer repents and prays continually for the victim, both parties gain and become like siblings. In compensation for a lost family member, they gain several new ones. Submitting to the Divine Destiny and Decree, they abandon enmity. Especially if they have taken part in the *Risale-i Nur*'s teachings, individual and collective peace and brotherhood in the *Risale-i Nur*'s circle require that they put aside all grudges.

In Denizli prison, all prisoners who had been enemies became brothers via the *Risale-i Nur*. This was one of the reasons for our acquittal. Even the irreligious criminals said about us: "How wonderful! How blessed they are!" All prisoners began going out for fresh air. However, I have seen here that a hundred men suffer because of one man, and do not go out to enjoy the fresh air together. Believers with sound consciences do not harm other believers because of some insignificant and minor error or advantage. If they make a mistake and cause harm, they should repent immediately.

The necessity of brotherhood among prisoners

In His Name, All-Glorified is He.

There is not a thing but it glorifies Him with praise.

Upon you be peace and God's mercy and blessing.

My dear new brothers and old prisoners!

I am convinced that Divine Favor placed us among you for a specific purpose relating to you: The *Risale-i Nur*, with its consolation and the truths of belief, is meant to save you from imprisonment's distress and a great deal of the worldly harm thereof. It is also meant to save your life, which otherwise would be wasted in grief and sorrow, to save you from moaning in both worlds.

If this is so, you obviously should be brothers to each other, after the example of the Denizli prisoners and the *Risale-i Nur* students. You see that guardians search through everything—food, bread, and so on—coming to you from the outside, so that you cannot use a slipped-in knife to attack each other. Besides, the guards who faithfully serve you suffer much trouble. You are not allowed to go outside together for fresh air because they think that you may attack each other like wild beasts.

Now, you new friends who are by nature heroic and courageous, you should display an example of spiritual valor and tell the prison's administrative board: "Even if we were given guns and revolvers, instead of knives, and ordered to use them, we would not hurt our unfortunate friends who suffer as we do. We are determined to forgive them and not to offend them, regardless of our former reasons for hostility, for these are requirements of belief and Islamic brotherhood, in our interests, and commanded by the Qur'an.

By this means and attitude, you may transform this prison into a blessed place of study.

An important matter

I will explain briefly a comprehensive truth that occurred to my heart on *Laylatu'l-Qadr* (the Night of Power and Destiny).[8] The Second World War was a display of extreme tyranny and injustice that entailed ruthless destruction. Countless innocent people were ruined due to one criminal. The defeated were led to awesome despair, while the victors worried about keeping their supremacy. Many suffer ghastly pangs of conscience because they could not repair the destruction they caused. The war showed just how transitory worldly life is, how deceitful modern civilization's frivolities are. The war gravely

---

[8] *Laylatu'l-Qadr*, to which the Qur'an refers in 97:1–5, is the most sacred night of the year. According to the majority of scholars, it is the 27th night of Ramadan. The Qur'an says concerning it: *Laylatu'l-Qadr is better than a thousand months. The angels and the Spirit descend in it by the permission of their Lord with His decrees for every affair—being a pure mercy and security, being until the rise of the dawn.* (97:3–5) (Tr.)

and extensively damaged human nature's essence and exalted potential. In some places, heedlessness, misguidance, and gross naturalism have been smashed by the Qur'an's diamond sword, while it has unveiled the extreme ugliness and cruelty of the true face of world politics, the most extensive, suffocating, and deceiving reflection of heedlessness and misguidance.

All this proves that since the worldly life, of which humanity is enamored, is ugly and transitory, human true, conscious nature will search with all its strength for eternal life, for which it truly yearns and loves. Signs have already appeared in the North, the West, and the United States. The Qur'an of miraculous exposition, which has had countless students for over thirteen centuries, every truth of which has been confirmed by innumerable truthful scholars, and which has remained alive in the minds of millions of its memorizers with all its holiness, teaches and proclaims the eternal life, explicitly or implicitly, in many of its powerful, striking, and reiterated verses. It instructs people in its particular tongues and, in a way unmatched by any other book, conveys the good news of eternal life and everlasting happiness, healing all our wounds. Given this, and provided that humanity does not lose its ability to reason or suffer complete physical or spiritual destruction, the vast masses and great states will search out the Qur'an of miraculous exposition. Having perceived its truths, they will become devoted to it heart and soul, just as some famous preachers in Sweden, Norway, Finland, and England, and a significant community in the United States in quest of the true religion, have shown an inclination to accept it. This will take place because the Qur'an has no equal, and nothing can take the place of this greatest miracle.

We also may say that among many other useful books and compilations, the *Risale-i Nur* has performed a service like a diamond sword in the hand of this Greatest Miracle, and that it silences even its most stubborn enemies. Having originated in the Qur'an, the *Risale-i Nur* explains and offers the Qur'anic truths in a way that enlightens the mind, soul, and feelings. It heals those wounded by modern trends, and defeats heretics and their anti-Qur'an propaganda. Many of its treatises, such as "The Treatise of Nature," "The Staff of Moses," and "The Fruits of Belief," have smashed naturalism and scientific materialism, the most formidable fortification of misguidance. They have banished heedlessness in its most dense, suffocating, and extensive dimensions, all of which evolved under the broad veil of scientism, by demonstrating the light of Divine Unity in a most radiant fashion.

The Fourteenth Word

A warning lesson for my heedless soul

In the Name of God, the All-Merciful, the All-Compassionate.

The worldly life is but a transient enjoyment of delusion. (3:185)

Y WRETCHED SOUL, SUNK IN HEEDLESSNESS, WHICH SEES THIS LIFE AS sweet and, oblivious of the Hereafter, seeks it alone! You resemble an ostrich that, seeing the hunter and unable to escape by flying away, sticks its head in the sand so that the hunter may not see it. However, its huge body remains in the open, so of course the hunter can see it. Only the ostrich's eyes are closed in the sand, and so it cannot see the hunter.

O my soul! Consider the following comparison and understand how focusing only on this world changes a great pleasure into a grievous pain:

Imagine that there are two people in this village (Barla). Ninety-nine out of every hundred of one's friends have moved to Istanbul, where they are living happily. He will shortly join them, and so longs for and thinks of Istanbul. When he is told he can go there, he will be overjoyed and go happily. The second person, facing the same situation, thinks that some of his friends have perished and that the others have gone where they do not see and cannot be seen. Imagining that they have gone to utter misery, he seeks consolation in his only remaining friend, who is about to get ready. He wants to compensate for the heavy pangs of separation through that friend.

O my soul! God's Beloved above all, Prophet Muhammad, upon him be peace and blessings, and all your friends are on the other side of the grave. One or two remain here, but they also will go there. So do not fear death or the grave, or avert your attention from death. Look at it bravely and listen to what it seeks. Laugh in its face and see what it wants. And be sure that you are not like the second person.

O my soul! Do not say: "Times have changed. This age is different, for everyone is plunged into this world and adores this life. Everyone is openly committed to the struggle for livelihood." For death does not change. Separation does not end and become eternal union or companionship. Our intrinsic impotence and poverty do not change; rather, they increase. Our journey (through this world) is not cut; rather, it becomes faster.

Do not say: "I am like everyone else." Everyone befriends you only as far as the grave. The consolation of everyone suffering the same misfortune cannot help you on the other side. Neither imagine that you are free and independent. Look at this temporary world with the eye of wisdom. See that everything has an order and purpose. How can you be left to yourself, for this would place you outside the order and cause you to be without purpose. All those events like earthquakes are not playthings of chance.

You see the earth's extremely well-designed and finely embroidered clothes, which it is dressed in one over and within the other, and all plant and animal species are adorned and decked out from top to bottom with important purposes and instances of wisdom. It is turned like an ecstatic Mevlevi dervish in perfect order and for exalted aims. So how can you suppose its vital, death-bringing events, like the recent earthquake,[9] which may be understood as the earth's shaking off the weight of certain forms of human heedlessness of which it does not approve—especially in believers—to be without purpose and the result of chance? How can you, by showing the grievous losses of those affected by such events as unrecompensed and as having gone for nothing, throw them into a dreadful despair? People who do so are committing a great error and a great wrong.

Such events happen at the command of One All-Wise and All-Compassionate so that what the believers lose via such events might become just as worthy of reward as alms and thereby gain permanence. This loss is also an atonement for those sins arising from ingratitude for Divine bounties.

A day will come when this subjugated earth will see our works, which are the adornments of its face, tainted by associating partners with God and without the necessary gratitude. It will disapprove of them and, when the Creator commands, will wipe them off its face and cleanse it. At God's command, it will pour those who associate partners with God into Hell and say to the thankful: "Come and enter Paradise."

---

[9] It refers to the 1935 earthquake in Izmir, Turkey. (Tr.)

The Seventeenth Word

The meaning of worldly life, and remedies for worldly misfortune

In the Name of God, the All-Merciful, the All-Compassionate.

We have made all that is on the earth an ornament for it that We may test them: which of them is best in conduct. Yet, We surely reduce all that is on it a barren dust-heap. (18:7–8)

The present, worldly life is but a play and pastime. (6:32)

[NOTE: This Word consists of two exalted Stations and an Addendum of signal importance.]

The first station

 THE ALL-COMPASSIONATE CREATOR, ALL-MUNIFICENT PROVIDER, All-Wise Maker shapes this world as a festival, a place of celebration for spirits and spirit beings. He has decorated it with His Names' most wonderful inscriptions, and clothes each spirit in a body equipped with suitable and appropriate senses so that it may benefit from the innumerable good things and bounties therein. He gives each spirit a corporeal body and sends it to this spectacle once.

He divides the festival, which in terms of time and space is very extensive, into centuries, years, seasons, and days, and into certain parts. Each one is an exalted festival during which all animate beings and plants parade. Especially in spring and summer, the earth's surface is a vast series of festivals for small creatures, an arena so glittering and attractive that it draws the gaze of angels and the heavens' other inhabitants, and spirit beings in the higher abodes. For those who think and reflect, it is an arena for reflection so wonderful that we cannot describe it appropriately.

However, the displays of the Divine Names the All-Merciful and the Giver of Life in this Divine festival are counterbalanced by the Names the All-Overwhelming and All-Crushing, and the One Who Causes to Die via death and separation. This does not seem to be in line with the all-embracing Mercy expressed in: *My Mercy encompasses all things* (7:156). Nevertheless it is so in several ways, one of which is as follows:

After each group has completed its turn of parade and the desired results have been obtained, the All-Munificent Maker, the All-Compassionate Creator, causes most of them, by His Compassion, to feel weariness and distaste for the world. He grants them a desire for rest and a longing to emigrate to another world. Thus, when they are to be discharged from life's duties, He arouses in them an enthusiastic inclination to return to their original home.

The All-Merciful One bestows martyrdom on soldiers who die in the course of duty (defending their sacred values), and rewards the cattle sacrificed for His sake with an eternal corporeal existence in the Hereafter, and with the rank of being mount for their owner on the Bridge[10]—like *Buraq*.[11] Therefore, it is not far from His infinite Mercy that other animate beings who die and suffer while performing their God-given duties, in accord with their nature and obedience to the Divine commands, should receive a spiritual reward and wage according to their capacities from His Mercy's inexhaustible treasuries. So, they should not be resentful of their departure from this world; rather, they should be pleased. *Only God knows the Unseen.*

Humanity, being the most honored of animate beings, is the greatest beneficiary of these festivals and the most enamored of and immersed in the world. So, when death approaches, God, out of His Mercy, gives each person a mood whereby he or she feels distaste with this world and longs to go to the eternal world. Whoever is not lost in misguidance benefits from this mood and dies with a tranquil heart. I will give five of the many reasons leading to this mood:

ONE: Due to old age, the All-Merciful One shows the stamp of transience and decline on that which is beautiful and tempting in this world, as

---

[10] See ad-Daylami, *al-Musnad*, 1:85. (Tr.)

[11] The heavenly mount that bore the Prophet through the heavens during his Ascension. (Tr.)

well as the bitter meaning they have. By causing us to become dissatisfied with the world, He causes us to seek a permanent beloved.

Two: Ninety-nine percent of our friends have died and gone to the other world. By engendering within us a longing for the same place through that heart-felt attachment, He enables us to meet death with joy.

Three: By causing us to feel our inherent infinite weakness and impotence and thereby to understand the great weight of our life's burdens and responsibilities, He implants within us a great wish for rest and a sincere longing to go to another world.

Four: He shows believers through the light of belief that death is a change of abode, not an eternal execution; that the grave is the door to illuminated worlds, not the mouth of a dark well; and that for all its glitter this world is like a dungeon when compared to the Hereafter. Therefore, to leave this dungeon for the gardens of Paradise, and pass from the troublesome turmoil of bodily life to the world of rest and the realm where spirits soar, and to slip free of the distressing noise of creatures and go to the All-Merciful's Presence is a journey and a happiness to be desired most earnestly.

Five: By revealing to those who give ear to the Qur'an the knowledge of truth it contains, as well as the world's true nature through the light of truth, He explains that love for and attachment to this world are meaningless, for:

- The world is a book of the Eternally Besought One. Its letters and words point to Another's Essence, Names, and Attributes. So learn and adopt its meaning, abandon its decorations, and go.

- The world is a tillage; sow it, harvest your crop, and preserve it. Throw away the chaff, and give it no importance.

- The world is a collection of mirrors that continuously pass on, one after the other. Know the One Who is manifest in them, see His lights, understand the manifestations of the Names appearing in them, and love the One they signify. End your attachment for those fragments of glass, which are doomed to be broken and perish.

- The world is a moving place of trade. Do your business and leave. Do not tire yourself by uselessly pursuing caravans that leave you behind.

- The world is a temporary place of recreation. Study it to learn what you need to know. Ignore its apparent, ugly face, but pay attention to its hidden, beautiful face, which looks to the Eternal All-Gracious

One. Go for a pleasant and beneficial visit and then come back. When the scenes displaying those fine views and beautiful things disappear, do not cry like a child, and do not be anxious.

• The world is a guest-house. Eat and drink within the limits set by the All-Munificent Host Who has built it, and offer thanks. Act and behave in accordance with His Law. Then leave and go away without looking back. Do not interfere in it; nor busy yourself in vain with things that leave you and do not concern you.

He shows the world's real character through such plain truths, and makes death less painful. Indeed, He makes death desirable to those awake to truth, and shows that everything He does has a trace of His Mercy. The Qur'an's verses also point to other particular reasons.

Woe to him who has no share of these five reasons or realities!

The second station

A supplication

O Lord. Heedlessly not trusting in You, but relying on my own power and will, I looked in all six directions for a cure to my pain. I found none. However, it occurred to me: "Isn't it enough for you that you have pains as cure?"

In heedlessness I looked to the past on my right to find solace. But yesterday appeared in the form of my father's grave, and the past as the huge tomb of my forefathers. Instead of consolation, it filled me with horror.*

*Belief shows that huge, terrifying tomb to be a familiar and illuminated meeting place for the gathering of friends.

I looked to the future on the left, but found no cure. Rather, tomorrow appeared in the form of my grave, and the future as the large tomb of my contemporaries and future generations. Instead of giving me relief, it scared me.*

*Belief and the peace it provides show that frightful large tomb to be a feast of the All-Merciful in delightful palaces of bliss.

As no good appeared from the left either, I looked at the present. I saw it like a coffin carrying my desperately struggling corpse.*

*Belief shows that coffin to be a place of business and a glittering guest-house.

Finding no cure in that direction either, I raised my head and looked at the top of the tree of my life. I saw that its single fruit was my corpse, looking down at me.*

*Belief shows that this fruit is not a corpse. In reality, it shows that the spirit, which is to be favored with eternal happiness in an eternal life, has left its worn-out home to travel among the stars.

Despairing of that direction too, I lowered my head and saw that the dust of my bones had mixed with the dust of my first creation. This only increased my pain.*

*Belief shows that dust to be the door to Mercy and the curtain over the windows of the hall of Paradise.

Turning away, I looked behind and saw a temporary world with no foundation revolving in valleys of nothingness and the darkness of non-existence. Giving no cure, it added more gloom and terror to my pain.*

*Belief shows that world to be the missives of the Eternally Besought One and sheets of Divine inscriptions. Having completed their duties and expressed their meanings, they leave their results behind for a new existence.

Since I saw no good from that direction either, I looked in front and saw the door of my grave standing open at the end. Behind it was the highway leading to eternity, which caught my eyes from afar.*

*Belief shows the grave to be the door to the world of light. As that way leads to eternal happiness, it cures my pain.

While looking in these six directions, I felt only horror and desolation. Apart from an insignificant free will, I have nothing with which to resist or oppose them.*

*Belief gives a document for relying on an Infinite Power in place of our willpower, which is like matter's smallest indivisible part. Indeed, belief itself is such a document.

Human free will lacks power, and its range is short and itself is inaccurate. Apart from serving as a tool to achieve human deeds [which God creates], it cannot do or create anything.*

*Belief causes the willpower to be used in God's name and makes it sufficient against whatever it faces. It is like a soldier who uses his insignificant power on the state's behalf being able to do far greater things than he could do on his own.

It can neither penetrate the past nor discern the future, and is of no benefit in regard to my ambitions and pains in regard to them.*

*Since belief takes its reins from the hand of the animal body and gives them to the heart and the spirit, it can penetrate the past and the future, for the heart's and spirit's sphere of life is broad.

Human willpower is active only in the brief present time and the passing present instant. I have infinite needs and an innate weakness. I am destitute and helpless. I am in a wretched state due to the terror and loneliness coming from the six directions. And yet infinite desire and ambition, inscribed on the page of my being by the Pen of Power, is embedded in my nature. Indeed, samples of everything in the universe are contained in my being. I am connected with all of them, and I work for them.

The sphere of need is as extensive as sight, and extends as far as the imagination. I need whatever I do not have, and so my need is limitless. Yet my power extends only as far as I can reach. Thus my wants and needs are infinite, while my capital is minute and insignificant. So, what does that insignificant willpower signify when confronted with such need? I have to search for another solution.

The solution is not to rely on our willpower, but to submit to the Divine Will and seek refuge in His Power by trusting in Him. "O Lord. Since this is the way of salvation, I give up my free will on Your way and abandon my ego.

I do this so that Your Grace may help and support me out of compassion for my impotence and weakness, that Your Mercy may take pity on me because of my want and need, and that It may be a support for me and open its door to me.

Whoever finds the boundless sea of Mercy does not rely on his own free will, which is no more than a drop of water seen in a mirage. He does not abandon Mercy and resort to his will.

Alas! We have been deceived. We thought that this worldly life is constant, and thus lost it thoroughly. Indeed, this passing life is but a sleep that passed like a dream. This life, having no foundation, flies like the wind. Those who rely on themselves and think they will live forever certainly will die. They race toward death, and this world, humanity's home, falls into the darkness of annihilation. Ambitions are time-bounded, but pains endure in the spirit.

Since this is the reality, come, my wretched soul that is fond of living and wants a long life, that loves the world and has boundless ambition and pain. Awaken and come to your senses. Consider that while the firefly relies on its own dim light and always remains in night's boundless darkness, the honeybee finds the sun of daytime and observes its friends (flowers) gilded with sunlight because it does not rely on itself. In the same way, if you rely on yourself, and your being and self-confidence, you will be like the firefly. But if you dedicate yourself, your transient being and body on the way of the Creator Who gave it to you, you will find, like the honeybee, an endless life of being. Dedicate it, for your being and your body is no more than a Divine trust to you.

Moreover, it is the Creator's property; it is He Who gave it to you. So use it for His sake unhesitatingly and without placing Him under obligation so that it will gain permanence. For a negation negated is an affirmation. Thus if our non-being is negated (in favor of Being), our being finds true existence. The All-Munificent Creator buys His own property from you. In return, He gives you a high price like Paradise, looks after it for you, and increases its value. He will return it to you in a perfected and permanent form. So, my soul, do not wait. Do this business, which is profitable in five respects. As well as being saved from five losses, make a fivefold profit in one transaction.[12]

"I love not those that set."

In the Name of God, the All-Merciful, the All-Compassionate.

But when it set, he said: "I love not those that set." (6:76)

This verse on the universe's decay, uttered by Prophet Abraham, upon him be peace, made me weep.

The eyes of my heart wept bitter tears for it. Each tear was so bitterly sad that it caused others to fall, as though the tears themselves were weeping. Those tears make up the lines that follow. They are like a commentary on the words of a wise Prophet contained in God's Word—the Qur'an.

A beloved who disappears is not beautiful, for one doomed to decline cannot be truly beautiful. It is not, and should not be, loved in the heart, for the heart is created for eternal love and is a mirror of the Eternally Besought One.

---

[12] Refer to The Sixth Word for the five profits or advantages and five losses. (Tr.)

A desired one doomed to set and disappear is unworthy of the heart's attachment or the mind's preoccupation. It cannot be the object of desire, and is unworthy of being missed with grief. So why should the heart adore and be attached to it?

One sought who is lost in decay and death—I do not desire such a one. For I am mortal and therefore do not seek or desire anything mortal.

One worshipped who is buried in death—I do not invoke or seek refuge with such a one. For I am infinitely needy and impotent. That which is powerless cannot cure my endless pain or solve my infinitely deep wounds. How can anything subject to decay be an object of worship?

A mind obsessed with appearances wails upon seeing that which it adores in the world decay and die, while the spirit, which seeks an eternal beloved, also wails, saying: "I love not those that set."

I do not want or desire separation, for I cannot endure it.

Meetings followed immediately by bitter separation are not worthy of thought or longing. For just as the disappearance of pleasure is pain, imagining it is also pain. The works of lovers, that is, the works of poetry on metaphorical love (love for the opposite sex), are lamentations caused by the pain arising from imagining this disappearance. If you condensed their spirit, this lament would flow from each.

Thus, it is due to the pain coming from such meetings and painful metaphorical loves that my heart cries out, like Abraham: "I love not those that set."

If you desire permanence in this transient world, permanence is born out of transience and annihilation. Annihilate your evil-commanding soul so that you may gain permanence.

Free yourself of bad morals, the basis of worldly adoration, and realize self-annihilation. Sacrifice your wealth in your possession and control for the True Beloved's sake. See the end of beings, which marks extinction. For the way leading from this world to permanence passes through self-annihilation.

The human mind, absorbed in causality, laments the upheavals caused by the world's decay. The conscience, desiring true existence, wails like Abraham: "I love not those that set." It severs its connection with metaphorical beloveds and decaying beings, and attaches itself to the Truly Existent One, the Eternal Beloved.

O my base soul. This world and all beings are mortal. However, you can find two ways to the All-Permanent Being in each mortal thing, and discern two gleams or mysteries of the manifestations of the Undying Beloved's Grace—if you sacrifice your mortal being.

The act of bestowing is discerned and the All-Merciful's favor is perceived in each bounty. If you discern this act through what is bestowed, you will find the All-Bestowing One. Each work of the Eternally Besought One points out the All-Majestic Maker's Names like a missive. If you understand the meaning through the inscription, the Names will lead you to the One called by those Names.[13] Since it is possible to find the kernel, the essence, of these transient things, obtain it. Discard their meaningless shells into the flood of mortality.

Every item that exists is a word of embodied meaning and shows many of the All-Majestic Maker's Names. Since beings are words of Divine Power, understand their meanings and place them in your heart. Fearlessly cast the letters left without meaning into the wind of transience and forget about them.

The worldly mind, preoccupied with appearances and whose capital consists only of knowledge of the material world, cries out in bewilderment and frustration, as its chains of thought end in nothingness and non-existence. It seeks a true way leading to truth. Since the spirit has withdrawn from what sets and is mortal and the heart has abandoned the deceiving beloveds, and since the conscience has turned away from transitory beings, you, my wretched soul, must seek help in: "I love not those that set," and be saved.

See how well Mawlana Jami',[14] who was intoxicated with the "wine" of love as if created from love, expressed it in order to turn faces from multiplicity to unity—the parenthetical additions belong to me:

---

[13] For example, through its coming into existence, beauty, shape, proportions, color, and the function it does, a flower displays the Divine Names the Maker, the All-Beautiful, the All-Shaping, the All-Just, the All-Coloring, and the All-Wise, respectively; and the Names point out the One Who has them. (Tr.)

[14] Mawlana Nuru'd-Din 'Abdu'r-Rahman ibn Ahmad al-Jami' (1414–1492 CE), commonly called Mulla Jami', is regarded as the last great classical poet of Persia, and a saint. His *Salaman and Absal* is an allegory of profane and sacred love. Some of his other works include *Haft Awrang*, *Tuhfatu'l-Ahrar*, *Layla wu Majnun*, *Fatihat ash-Shabab*, and *Lawa'ih*. (Tr.)

Want only One (the rest are not worth wanting).
Call One (the others do not come to your assistance).
Seek One (the others are not worth seeking).
See and follow One (the others are not seen all the time;
they become invisible behind the veil of mortality).
Know One (knowledge other than that which does not add to
your knowledge of Him is useless).
Mention One (words not concerning Him may be regarded as useless).

O Jami', I admit that you spoke the truth. The True Beloved, True Sought One, True Desired One, and True Object of Worship is He alone. In the mighty circle of remembering and reciting God's Names, this universe and its inhabitants declare, in various tongues and tones: "There is no deity but God," and testify to Divine Oneness. It salves the wound caused by those that set, and points to the Undying Beloved.

Depictions of the worlds of the rightly-guided and the heedless

(NOTE: About 25 years ago on Yuşa Tepesi in Beykoz, Istanbul, when I had decided to renounce the world, several important friends came to call me back to the world and my former position. I told them to leave me till the following morning so I could seek Divine guidance. That morning the following two "Tables," occurred to me. They resemble verse, but they are not. I have not changed them for the sake of that blessed memory. They are included here for they are appropriate.)

FIRST TABLE

(A depiction of the true spirit of the heedless people's world.)

Do not invite me to the world,
I came and found it evil and mortal.

Heedlessness was a veil;
I saw the light of truth concealed.

All things, the whole of creation—
I saw were mortal and full of harm.

Existence, indeed I put it on.
Alas! It was non-existence; I suffered much.

As for life, I experienced it;
I saw it was torment within torment.

Intellect became pure retribution;
I saw permanence to be tribulation.

Life was like a wind, it passed in whims;
I saw perfection to be pure loss.

Actions were only for show;
I saw ambition to be pure pain.

Union was in fact separation;
I saw the cure to be the ailment.

These lights became darkness;
I saw these friends to be orphans.

These voices were announcements of death;
I saw the living to be dead.

Knowledge changed into whim;
I saw in science thousands of ailments.

Pleasure became unmixed pain;
I saw existence to be compounded non-existence.

I have found the True Beloved;
Ah, I suffered much pain because of separation.

Second table

(This table describes the true spirit of the world of the people of guidance and peace.)

Heedlessness has disappeared;
I have seen the light of truth to be manifest.

Existence is a proof of Divine Being.
See, life is the mirror reflecting The Truth.

Intellect has become the key to treasuries.
See, mortality is the door to eternity.

The spark of self-attainment has died.
But see, there is the sun of grace and beauty.

Separation has become true union;
See, pain is pure pleasure.

Life has become pure action.
See, eternity is pure life.

Darkness is a thin membrane enclosing light.
See, there is true life in death.

All things have become familiar.
See, all sounds are the mentioning of God.

All the particles in creation:
See, each glorifies God and calls Him by His Names.

I have found poverty to be a treasury of wealth.
See, in impotence lies perfect power.

If you have found God,
See, all things are yours.

If you are a slave of the Owner of all things,
See, His property is yours.

If you are egotist and claim self-ownership,
See, it is endless trial and tribulation.

It is infinite torment, taste it,
See, it is an unbearable calamity.

If you are truly a slave of God, devoted to Him,
See, it is an infinite delight.

Taste its uncountable rewards,
See the boundless bliss; experience it.

O my soul! Like my heart weep, cry out and say:

I am mortal, so I do not want the mortal.
I am impotent, so I do not desire the impotent.
I surrendered my spirit to the All-Merciful, so I desire none else.
I want only one who will remain my friend forever.
I am but an insignificant particle, but I desire an everlasting sun.
I am nothing in essence, but I wish for the whole of creation.

The Twenty-third Word

Virtues of belief and remarks on our misery and happiness

(This Word consists of two Chapters.)

In the Name of God, the All-Merciful, the All-Compassionate.

Surely We have created humanity of the best stature as the perfect pattern of creation; then We reduced it to the lowest of the low, save those who believe and do good, rihgteous deeds. (95:4–5)

The first chapter

N THE FOLLOWING FIVE POINTS, WE WILL EXPLAIN FIVE OUT OF THE thousands of virtues of belief.

FIRST POINT: We reach the highest degree of perfection and become worthy of Paradise through the light of belief. The darkness of unbelief reduces us to the lowest level so that we deserve Hell. For belief connects us to our All-Majestic Maker, so belief is a relation and connection. Thus our value derives from the Divine art and the Divine Names that are manifested in us through belief. Unbelief breaks this relation, thereby veiling the Divine art and reducing our value to that of a mere physical entity. Since matter is perishable and physical life is no more than a transient animal life, our value as a physical entity is virtually nothing. We will explain this through a parable.

The value of the iron (or any other material) from which a work of art is made differs from the value of the art expressed in it. Sometimes they may have the same value, or the art's worth may be far more than its material, or vice versa. An antique may fetch a million dollars, while its material is not even worth a few cents. If taken to the antiques market, it may be sold for its true value because of its art and the brilliant artist's name. If taken to a blacksmith, it would be sold only for the value of its iron.

Similarly, each person is a unique, priceless work of God Almighty's Art. We are His Power's most delicate and graceful miracles, beings created to manifest all His Names and inscriptions in the form of a miniature specimen of the universe. If we are illuminated with belief, these meaningful inscriptions become visible, and believers read them consciously. They manifest these inscriptions through their connection with their Maker; that is, the Divine art contained in each person is revealed through such affirmations as: "I am the work of the All-Majestic Maker, the creature and object of His Mercy and Munificence." As a result, and because we gain value in proportion to how well we reflect this art, we move from insignificance (in material terms) to beings ranked above all creatures. We communicate with God, are His guests on the earth, and are qualified for Paradise.

However, should unbelief, which means the severance of this connection, is ingrained in us, all of the Divine Names' manifestations are veiled by darkness and thus non-expressive. For if the Artist is unknown, how can the aspects expressing the worth of His Art be identified? Thus most meaningful instances of that sublime Art and elevated inscriptions are concealed. As regards the material aspects of our being, unbelievers attribute them to physical causes, nature and chance, thereby reducing them to plain glass instead of sparkling diamonds. They are no more significant than any other material entity, self-condemned to a transient and suffocating life, and no better than a most impotent, needy, and afflicted animal that eventually will become dust. Unbelief thus spoils our nature by changing our diamond into coal.

SECOND POINT: Belief is a light. Just as it illuminates human beings and reveals all the messages inscribed in their being by the Eternally Besought One, it also illuminates the universe and removes darkness from the past and future as well. We will explain this truth through what I experienced regarding the meaning of: *God is the Guardian of those who believe. He brings them out of the layers of darkness into the light* (2:257).

I saw myself standing on an awe-inspiring bridge set over a deep valley between two mountains. The world was completely dark. Looking to my right, I imagined I saw a huge tomb in darkness. Looking to my left, I felt as if I were seeing violent storms and calamities being prepared amid the tremendous waves of darkness. Looking down, I imagined I saw a very deep precipice. I had a torch in the face of this terrifying darkness. I used it and could see a little with its light. A dreadful scene appeared to me in its dim light. All along the bridge were such horrible dragons, lions, and monsters that I wished I had no torch. Whichever way I directed it, I got the same fright. "This torch brings me only trouble," I exclaimed, angrily throwing it away and breaking it. Suddenly darkness was replaced by light, as if I had switched on a huge light by breaking my torch. I saw everything in its true nature.

I discovered that the bridge was a highway on a smooth plain. The huge tomb was a green, beautiful garden in which illustrious persons were leading assemblies of worship, prayer, glorification, and discourse. The turbulent, stormy, frightening precipices on my left appeared as a banqueting hall, a shaded promenade, a beautiful resting place behind lovely mountains. The horrible monsters and dragons were actually camels, oxen, sheep, and goats. "Praise and thanks be to God for the light of belief," I said, and then awoke reciting: *God is the Guardian of those who believe. He brings them out of the layers of darkness into the light.*

Thus, the two mountains are this life's beginning and end, that is, this world and the world of grave (between death and Resurrection). The bridge is the lifespan, between the two phases of the past (on the right) and the future (on the left). The torch is our conceited ego that, relying on its own achievements, ignores Divine Revelation. The monsters were the worlds' events and creatures.

Those who have fallen into the darkness of misguidance and heedlessness because of their confidence in their egos resemble me in the former state—in the dim light of a torch. With their inadequate and misguided knowledge, they see the past as a huge tomb in the darkness of extinction and the future as a stormy scene of terror controlled by coincidence or chance. The torch also shows them events and creatures, which are in reality dutiful servants or officials of the All-Wise and All-Merciful fulfilling specific functions and serve good purposes, as harmful monsters. These are the people referred to in: *As to those who do not believe, their guardians are powers of evil who institute patterns of belief and rule in defiance of God. They bring them out of the light into layers of darkness* (2:257).

If, however, people are favored with Divine guidance so that belief enters their hearts and their Pharaoh-like egos are broken, thereby enabling them to listen to the Book of God, they will resemble me in my later state.

Suddenly the universe will fill with Divine Light, demonstrating the meaning of: *God is the Light of the heavens and the earth* (24:35). Believers see in this light of belief or right guidance that the past is not a huge tomb; rather, each past century is the realm of authority of a Prophet or saints, where the purified souls, having completed the duties of their lives (worship) with: "God is the All-Great," flew to higher abodes on the side of the future. Looking to their left and through the light of belief, they discern, behind the mountain-like revolutions of the Intermediate World (the world of grave) and the next life, a feasting place set up by the All-Merciful at palaces of bliss in gardens of Paradise. They understand that storms, earthquakes, epidemics, and similar events serve a specific function, just as the spring rain and winds, despite their apparent violence, serve many agreeable purposes. They even see death as the beginning of eternal life, and the grave as the gateway to eternal happiness. You can deduce other realities in the light of the comparison.

THIRD POINT: Belief is both light and power. Those who attain true belief can challenge the universe and, in proportion to their belief's strength, be relieved of the pressures of events. Relying on God, they travel safely through the mountainous waves of events in the ship of life. Having entrusted their burdens to the Absolutely Powerful One's Hand of Power, they voyage through the world comfortably until their last day. The grave will be a resting place, after which they will fly to Paradise to attain eternal bliss. If, however, they do not rely upon God, their worldly life will force them down to the lowest depths. That means, belief requires affirming Divine Unity; affirmation of Divine Unity requires submitting to God; submission to God requires relying on God; and reliance on God yields happiness in both worlds. But do not misunderstand reliance on God; it does not mean ignoring cause and effect and complete negligence of the means to attain a goal. Rather, it means that one should think of causes or means as a veil before the Power's hand. One observes them by seeking to comply with the Divine Will, which is a sort of prayer in action. However, such desire and seeking is not enough to secure a particular effect. We must understand that, in accordance with right belief, the result is to be expected only from God, the All-Mighty. As He is the sole producer of effects, we always should be grateful to Him.

The one who relies on God and one who does not are like the two men in the following parable:

Once two people boarded a royal ship with heavy burdens. One put his burden on the deck immediately after boarding and sat on it to keep it safe. The other one, even after being told to lay his burden down, refused to do so and said: "I won't put it down, because it might get lost. Besides, I'm strong enough to carry it." He was told:

> This reliable royal ship, which carries us, is stronger and can hold it better. You will most probably get tired, feel dizzy, and fall into the sea with your burden. Your strength will fail, and then how will you bear this burden that gets heavier every moment? If the captain sees you in this state, he might say you are insane and expel you from the ship. Or maybe he will think you do not trust them and make fun of them, and he will order you to be imprisoned. Also, you will be marked out and become the butt of jokes. Your vanity reveals your weakness, your arrogance reveals your impotence, and your pretension betrays your humiliation. And so you have become a laughing-stock—look how everybody is laughing at you.

These words convinced him to follow his companion's example. He told him: "May God be pleased with you. I have obtained relief and am no longer subject to imprisonment or becoming a laughing-stock." So trust in God and come to your senses, as the man in the parable did. Put your trust in God and be delivered from begging from creation and trembling in fear at each happening. Doing so will deliver you from self-conceit, being ridiculous, the pressures of this life, and the torments of the Hereafter.

FOURTH POINT: Belief enables us to attain true humanity, to acquire a position above all other creatures. Thus, belief and prayer are our most fundamental and important duties. Unbelief, by contrast, reduces us to the state of a brutal but very impotent beast.

A decisive proof for this truth is the difference between how human beings and animals come into existence. Almost from the very moment of birth, an animal seems to have been trained and perfected its faculties somewhere else. Within a few hours or days or months, it can lead its life according to its particular rules and conditions. A sparrow or a bee, for example, acquires or is inspired with the skill and ability to integrate into its environment within a matter of twenty days, while it would take a person twenty years to do so. This means that an animal's basic obligation and essential role does not include seeking perfection through learning, progress through scientific knowledge, or prayer and petitioning for help by displaying their impotence. Rather, their sole purpose is to act within the bounds of their innate faculties, which is the mode of worship specified for them.

People, however, are born knowing nothing of life and their environment and so must learn everything. As we cannot do this even within twenty years, we must continue to learn until we die. We are sent here with so much weakness and inability that we might need as many as two years to learn how to walk. Only after fifteen years can we distinguish good and evil. Only by living in a society can we become smart enough to choose between what is beneficial and what is harmful.

Thus the essential and intrinsic duty of our existence is to seek perfection through learning and to proclaim our worship of and servanthood to God through prayer and supplication. It is to seek answers for such essential questions as: "Through whose compassion is my life so wisely administered? Through whose generosity am I being so affectionately trained? Through whose favors and benevolence am I being so solicitously nourished?" It is to pray and petition the Provider of Needs in humble awareness of our needs, even a thousandth of which we cannot satisfy on our own. In short, it is flying to the highest rank of being worshipful servants of God on the wings of consciousness of our innate impotence and poverty.

And so our purpose here is to seek perfection through knowledge and prayer. Everything is, by its nature, essentially dependent on knowledge. And the basis, source, light, and spirit of all true knowledge is knowledge of God, of which belief is the very foundation. After belief, prayer is our essential duty and the basis of worship, for despite our infinite impotence, we are exposed to endless misfortune and innumerable enemies, and despite our infinite poverty, we suffer limitless need and demands.

Children express their need for something they cannot reach with words or tears. Both are a sort of plea or prayer, in word or deed, with the tongue of weakness. Eventually they get what they want. Similarly, we are quite like a beloved child in the world of living beings, who should either weep at the All-Merciful and Compassionate's Court through our weakness and impotence, or pray through to our poverty and need, so that our need may be satisfied. In return, we should perform our duty of gratitude and thanksgiving for this provision. Otherwise, the ingratitude of those who claim to have so much intelligence and power over everything that they can meet their own needs finally will come to the point where they resemble mischievous, lazy children moaning about irritating flies. Such ingratitude is against our essential nature and makes us worthy of severe punishment.

Fifth point: Belief requires prayer for attainment and perfection, and our essence needs it. God Almighty says: *Say (O Muhammad): "My Lord would not concern Himself with you but for your prayer"* (25:77), and: *Pray to Me and I will answer you* (40:60).

Question: If you say that you pray so many times but that your prayers are unanswered, despite the assurance given in the above verse, the answer would be as follows:

The Answer: An answered prayer does not necessarily mean its acceptance. There is an answer for every prayer. However, accepting the prayer and giving what is requested depends upon the All-Mighty's Wisdom. For example, a sick child asks a doctor for a certain medicine. The doctor will give either what is asked for or something better, or he will not give anything. It all depends upon how the medicine will affect the child. Similarly the All-Mighty, Who is the All-Just and Omnipresent, answers His servants' prayer and changes their loneliness into the pleasure of His company. But His answer does not depend on the individual's fancies; rather, according to His Wisdom, He gives what is requested, what is better, or nothing at all.

Moreover, prayer is a form of worship and worship is rewarded mainly in the Hereafter. Worldly needs and purposes are only causes or occasions for prayer. For example, praying for rain is a kind of worship occasioned by the lack of rain. If rain is the prayer's only aim, the prayer is unacceptable, for it is not sincere or intended to please God and obtain His approval.

Sunset determines the time for the evening Prayer, while solar and lunar eclipses occasion two particular kinds of worship. Since such eclipses—the veiling of two luminous signs of day and night—are two means of manifesting Divine Majesty, the All-Mighty calls His servants to perform a form of worship—the Prayer of Eclipse—particular to these occasions. This Prayer has nothing to do with causing the eclipse to end, for this is known already through astronomical calculations. Similarly, drought and other calamities are occasions for certain kinds of prayer. At such times, we best realize our impotence and so feel the need to take refuge in the high Presence of the Absolutely Powerful One through prayer and supplication.

If a calamity is not lifted despite many prayers, we should not say that the prayer has not been accepted. Rather, we should say that the time for prayer has not yet ended. If God removes the calamity because of His endless Grace and Munificence, this is light upon light, profit upon profit, and marks the end of the special occasion for prayer.

Praying is a mystery of servanthood to God through worship. Worship is done solely to please God and for His Sake. We should affirm and display our poverty and weakness, and seek refuge with Him through prayer. We must not interfere in His Lordship, but rather let God do as He wills. We must rely on His Wisdom and not accuse His Mercy.

Every creature offers its unique praise and worship to God. What reaches the Court of God from the universe is prayer.

- One kind of prayer is that which is done through the tongue of potential. Plants pray through the tongue of their potential to achieve a full form and manifest certain Divine Names.

- Another kind of prayer is expressed in the tongue of natural needs. All living beings ask the Absolutely Generous One to meet their vital needs, as they cannot do so on their own.

- Yet another kind of prayer is done in the tongue of complete helplessness. A living creature in straitened circumstances takes refuge in its Unseen Protector with a genuine supplication and turns to its All-Compassionate Lord. These three kinds of prayer are always acceptable, unless somehow impeded.

- The fourth type of prayer is the one done by humanity. This type falls into two categories: active and by disposition, and verbal and with the heart. For example, acting in accordance with causes or fulfilling the prerequisites is an active prayer. We try to gain God's approval by complying with causes or fulfilling the prerequisites, for causes alone or the fulfillment of prerequisites cannot produce the result—only God can do that. For example, plowing the soil is an active prayer, for this means knocking at the door of the treasury of God's Mercy. Such a prayer is usually acceptable, for it is an application to the Divine Name the All-Generous.

The second type of prayer of humanity, done with the tongue and the heart, is the ordinary one. This means that we ask God from the heart for something we cannot reach. Its most important aspect and finest and sweetest fruit is that we know that God hears us, is aware of our heart's contents, that His Power extends everywhere, that He can satisfy every desire, and that He comes to our aid out of mercy for our weakness and inadequacy.

And so, O helpless and poor person. Never abandon prayer, for it is the key to the Treasury of Mercy and the means of gaining access to the Infinite Power. Hold on to it. Ascend to the highest rank of humanity and, as creation's most favored and superior member, include the whole universe's prayer in your prayer. Say, on behalf of all beings: *From You alone do we seek help* (1:5), and become a beautiful pattern for creation.

The second chapter

(Five remarks on human happiness and misery)

[Human beings have been created of the best stature as the perfect pattern of creation, and given a comprehensive potential. They have been sent to the world as miracles of power, the ultimate pinnacle of creation, and wonders of art. For them, this world is arena of trial, where the two ways are open before them, one leading to infinite ascent, the other to infinite descent. So, by following either of these ways, they either will rise to the highest of the high or descend to the lowest of the low. I will expound the mystery of humanity's ascent and descent in five remarks.]

FIRST REMARK: We have some relationship with and are in need of most species. Our needs range into all parts of the universe, and our desires range as far as eternity. We desire a single flower as well as a whole spring, a garden as well as an eternal Paradise. We long to see our friend as well as the All-Beautiful, Gracious One of Majesty. As we have to knock on our beloved friend's door for a visit, so too in order to be able to rejoin the ninety-nine percent of our friends, who have left for the Intermediate World, and be saved from eternal separation, we also need to seek refuge at the Court of the Absolutely Powerful One, Who will close this huge world's door and open the door of the Hereafter, the world of wonders, and will replace this world with the next one.

Given this, our true object of worship can only be an All-Powerful One of Majesty, All-Compassionate One of Beauty and Grace, All-Wise One of Perfection, in Whose hand are the reins of all things, in Whose possession is the provision of every existence, Who sees everything and is omnipresent, unbounded by space, and free of any constraint, flaw, defect, and deficiency. For only One with infinite power and all-encompassing knowledge can satisfy our unlimited need and therefore it is only He Who is worthy of worship.

So, O humanity! If you worship Him alone, you will attain a rank above all other creatures. If you do not, you will become a disgraced slave to impotent creation. If you rely upon your selfhood and power instead of prayer and trust in God, and claim an arrogant superiority, you will become lower than a bee or an ant and weaker than a fly or a spider with respect to positive acts and constructive invention. But your evil and destruction will weigh heavier than a mountain and be more harmful than a pestilence.

So, O humanity! You have two aspects of being. One is positive and active, and has to do with constructive invention, existence, and goodness. The other is negative and passive, and concerns destruction, nonexistence, and evil. As for the first aspect of your being, you cannot compete with a bee or a sparrow, are weaker than a fly or a spider, and cannot achieve what they can. As for the second aspect of your being, however, you can surpass mountains, the earth, and the heavens, for you can bear a burden that they cannot. Thus your acts have a wider impact than theirs. When you do something good or build something, it reaches only as far as your hand and strength. But your evil and destructive acts are aggressive and expandable.

For example, unbelief is an evil, an act of destruction, an absence of affirmation. It may look like a single sin, but it implies an insult to creation, the debasement of all Divine Names, and the degradation of all humanity. For creation has a sublime rank and important task, for each part of it is a missive of the Lord, a mirror of His Glory, and a dutiful servant of His Divinity. Unbelief denies them this rank bestowed on them by virtue of these functions and reduces them to playthings of chance, and insignificant, useless, and worthless objects doomed to decay and decomposition.

Unbelief is also an insult to the Divine Names, Whose beautiful inscriptions and manifestations are seen in the mirrors of all created forms throughout the universe. Furthermore, it casts humanity down to a level more wretched and weak, helpless and destitute, than the lowliest animal. It reduces us to an ordinary, perishable sign-board without meaning, confused and swiftly decaying. And this when humanity, in reality, is a poetic work of Wisdom that manifests all Divine Names; a great miracle of Power that, like a seed, contains the Tree of Creation; and God-appointed ruler of the earth, who is superior to angels and higher than mountains, the earth, and heavens by virtue of the Supreme Trust we accepted.

In short: As regards evil and destruction, the carnal, evil-commanding soul may commit countless crimes and cause unlimited destruction, while its capacity to do good is very limited. It can destroy a house in a day but cannot rebuild it in a hundred days. But if it abandons self-reliance and vanity and relies upon Divine aid to do good and constructive things, if it abandons evil and destruction and seeks Divine forgiveness and so becomes a perfect servant of God, it becomes the referent of: *God will change their evil deeds into good deeds* (25:70). That is, our infinite capacity for evil is changed into an infinite ability for good. We attain the worth of "the perfect pattern of creation" and rise to the "highest of the high."

Consider then, O heedless one, the All-Mighty's Grace and Munificence. In reality, it is absolute justice to record one sin as a thousand sins, [due to its consequences and effects,] and a good act as only one. But God does the reverse: He records a sinful act as one and an act of goodness as ten, seventy, seven hundred, or, in some cases, seven thousand. From this we can understand that entering Hell is the result of one's deeds and pure justice, while entering Paradise is the result of His absolute Grace.

SECOND REMARK: Human beings have two faces. The first face looks to this worldly life because of our selfhood. Here our capital consists of a free will as feeble as a hair, a power restricted to a most limited talent with respect to positive, constructive acts, a life or lifespan as short as a flash of light, and a material existence bound to decompose swiftly. In this state, we are no more than a feeble member of one species among countless others spread throughout the universe.

The second face looks to the eternal life because of our nature as God's servants charged with and in need of worshipping Him. Our perception of helplessness and insufficiency as God's servants needy of Him make us extremely important and inclusive beings. For the All-Wise Originator has implanted an infinite impotence and poverty in our nature so that each of us may be a comprehensive mirror reflecting the boundless manifestations of an All-Compassionate One of infinite Power, an All-Munificent One of infinite Richness.

We resemble seeds. A seed is endowed with great potential by Divine Power and a subtle program by Divine Destiny, so that it may germinate underground, emerge from that narrow world and enter the spacious world of air. Asking its Creator in the tongue of its capacity to become a tree, it may attain a perfection particular to it. If, due to its malignant disposition, the seed abuses its potential to attract harmful substances, it will soon rot away in its narrow place. If it uses its potential properly, however, and in compliance with the creational commands of *The Splitter of grain and fruit-stone* (6:95), it will emerge from its narrow place and grow into an awesome, fruitful tree. In addition, its tiny and particular nature will come to represent a great and universal truth.

In just the same way, our essence is equipped by Power with great potential and is inscribed by Destiny with important programs. If we use our potential and faculties in this narrow world under the soil of worldly life to satisfy the fancies of our carnal, evil-commanding soul, we will, like a rotten seed, decay and decompose for an insignificant pleasure in a short life amidst hardships and troubles. Thus we will depart from this world with a heavy spiritual burden on our unfortunate souls.

But if we germinate the seed of our potential under the "soil of worship" with the "water of Islam" and the "light of belief" according to the Qur'an's decrees, and use our faculties for their true purposes, we will grow into eternal, majestic trees whose branches extend into the Intermediate World and the World of Representations or Immaterial Forms, and which will be favored with countless bounties and yield innumerable fruits of perfection in the next world and Paradise. We will, in fact, become the blessed, luminous fruit of the tree of creation.

True progress is possible only when we turn our faculties (e.g., intellect, heart, spirit, and even imagination) to the eternal life and make them occupied with its own kind of worship. What the misguided consider progress—being immersed in the life of this world and subjecting all our faculties to the carnal, evil-commanding selfhood to taste all worldly pleasures down to the basest—is nothing but decline and degradation. I once observed this truth in a vision, which is as follows:

I reached a huge city full of large palaces. Outside some of them, I noticed ongoing spectacles and shows to amuse and entertain. As I drew near to one of them, I saw that its owner was playing with a dog at the door. Women were chatting with young strangers, and young girls were organizing children's games. The doorman was behaving as if he were their master. I realized that the palace was empty, with all important tasks left unattended, for its corrupted inhabitants were pursuing useless affairs.

I then came across another palace. A faithful dog was lying at the door, and beside it was a doorman with a stern, serious, and sober expression. The palace seemed so quiet that I entered in wonder and amazement. Inside was a scene of great activity: one flour above another, the inhabitants were engaged in different, important tasks. The people on the first floor were managing the palace. On the second floor, girls and boys were studying. The women on the third floor were producing beautiful works of art and delicate embroidery. On the top floor, the owner was in constant communication with the king to secure his household's well-being and so that he could perform noble duties for his own progress and perfection. As they did not see me, I walked about unhindered.

Then I came out and looked around. I saw that the city was full of similar palaces. I asked and was told that the palaces like the first one belonged to the foremost unbelievers and misguided, while those of the second type belonged to upright Muslim notables. In one corner, I came across a palace on which my name was written: "Said." As I looked at it closely, I felt as if I saw my image on it. Crying in bewilderment, I came to my senses and awoke.

The city is our social life and the terrain of human civilization. Each palace is a human being, and the inhabitants are human senses and faculties (e.g., eyes, ears, intellect, heart and spirit, and powers of anger and lust). Each sense and faculty has a particular duty of worship, as well as particular pleasures and pains. The carnal soul and fancies, as well as the powers of anger and lust, correspond to the dog and the doorman. Thus, subjugating the sublime senses and faculties to carnal desires and fancies so that they forget their essential duties is decline and corruption. It certainly is not progress. You may interpret the other details for yourself.

THIRD REMARK: With respect to our constructive actions and bodily endeavors, we are like weak animals and helpless creatures. The realm at our disposal is so limited that our fingers can touch its circumference. Our weakness, impotence, and indolence are so great that even domesticated animals are influenced by them. If a domesticated animal is compared with its undomesticated counterpart, great differences can be seen.

But as recipient beings conscious of our need to pray and petition, we are honored, worthy travelers allowed to stay for a while in the guest-house of this world. We are guests of such a Munificent One that He has put His infinite treasuries of Mercy at our disposal and subjugated His unique works of creative Power and special servants to us. Also, He has prepared for our use, pleasure and recreation such a vast arena that its radius is as far as sight or even imagination can reach.

If we rely on our physical and innate abilities, taking the worldly life as our goal and focusing on its pleasures in pursuit of our livelihood, we will suffocate within a very narrow circle. Moreover, our bodily parts, senses, and faculties will bring suit and witness against us in the Hereafter. But if we know that we are guests and so spend our lives within the limits established and approved by our All-Munificent Host, we will lead a happy and peaceful life in a broad sphere and gain a long, eternal life. We can rise to the highest of the high, and all of our bodily members and faculties will testify in our favor in the Hereafter.

Our wonderful faculties are not meant for this trivial worldly life; rather, they are for our eternal life of great significance. For when compared with animals, we see that we are far richer than animals in respect of faculties and senses, while in regard to worldly pleasures and animal life we fall a hundred times lower. This is because every worldly pleasure we taste bears many traces of pain. Pains of the past, fears of the future and the pains at the cessation of every pleasure spoil our enjoyment. However, animals experience pleasure without pain, enjoyment without anxiety, and are neither wounded by the pains of the past nor distressed by the fears of the future. They enjoy comfortable lives and praise their Creator.

This means that if humanity, created of the best stature as the perfect pattern of creation, concentrates on this worldly life, we are far lower than a sparrow, although we have far more developed faculties than any animal. In order to explain this reality, I will repeat a parable which I wrote in another treatise.

A man gives his servant ten gold coins and tells him to have a suit made out of a particular cloth. He gives another servant a thousand gold coins and sends him to the market with a shopping list. The former buys an excellent suit of the finest cloth. The latter acts foolishly, for he neither notices how much money he was given nor reads the shopping list. Thinking that he should imitate his friend, he goes to a shop and asks for a suit. The dishonest shopkeeper gives him a suit of the very worst-quality cloth. The unfortunate servant returns to his master and receives a severe reprimand and a terrible punishment. Anyone can see that the thousand gold coins were not given for a suit, but for a very important transaction.

In the same way, our spiritual faculties, feelings, and senses are much more developed than those of animals. For example, we can see all degrees of beauty, distinguish all the varieties of the particular tastes of foods, penetrate the many details of realities, yearn for all ranks of perfection, and so on. But animals, with the exception of a particular faculty that reaches a high state of development according to its particular duty, can realize only slight development, if any.

We are rich in faculties because our senses and feelings have developed a great deal owing to our mind and intellect. Our many needs have caused us to evolve different types of emotions and to become very sensitive to many things. Also, due to our comprehensive nature we have been given desires turned to several aims and objectives. Our senses and faculties have greatly expanded due to the diversity of our essential duties. Furthermore, since we are inclined and able to worship, we have the potential to realize all kinds of perfection.

Such rich faculties and abundant potentialities cannot have been given to us for an insignificant, temporary, worldly life. In reality, they were given to us because our essential duty is to perceive our obligations, which are directed toward endless aims; to affirm our impotence, poverty, and insufficiency in the form of worship; to study creation's glorifications of God with our far-reaching sight and penetrating understanding, and to bear witness to them; to discern and be grateful for the All-Merciful One's aid sent in the form of bounties; and to gaze, reflect upon, and draw warnings from the miracles of His Power as manifested in creation.

O world-adoring one charmed by the worldly life and ignorant of the meaning of your nature as the perfect pattern of creation! Once I saw the true nature of this worldly life in a vision, as follows:

I found myself a traveler going on a long journey. My lord who set me making this journey gradually gave me some of the sixty gold coins He had allotted to me. This went on for some time, and after a while I arrived at an inn that provided some entertainment. In one night I spent ten gold coins on gambling and entertainment, and in pursuit of fame. The next morning, I had no money left. Nor could I do trade and buy provisions I would need at my destination. All I had left was pain, sorrow, and regret left by sins and illicit pleasures. While I was in this wretched state, a man appeared and said to me: "You have lost all you had and deserve to be punished. Moreover, you will go on to your destination with no money. But if you use your mind, the door of repentance is not closed. When you gradually receive the remaining fifteen gold coins, keep half in reserve and use it to buy what you will need at your destination."

My soul did not agree, so the man said: "Save a third of them then." Still my soul balked. The man insisted: "Then a quarter." I saw that my soul could not abandon its addictions, so the man turned away indignantly and disappeared. At once, I found myself on a high-speed train travelling through a tunnel. I was alarmed, but there was no escape. To my surprise, I saw very attractive flowers and tasty-looking fruits alongside the track, hanging out from the sides of the tunnel. I foolishly tried to pick some of them. But all around them were thorns that, due to the train's speed, tore at my hands and made them bleed. They cost me very much. Suddenly an attendant came and said: "Give me five cents and I'll give you as many flowers and fruits as you want. With your hands all cut up, you are losing a hundred instead of five cents. Besides, there is a punishment for picking them without permission."

Depressed by this condition, I looked out the window to see when the tunnel would end. But there was no end in sight. The tunnel's walls had many openings into which passengers were being thrown. Suddenly I caught sight of an opening just opposite me with a gravestone on either side. When I peered out, I made out my name, "Said," written in capital letters on a gravestone. I gave a cry of bewilderment and repentance. Unexpectedly, I heard the voice of the man who had advised me at the inn, asking: "Have you come to your senses?" I replied: "Yes, but I've been left powerless, and there is nothing I can do." He told me to repent and trust in God, to which I replied that I would. Then I woke up and I found myself transformed into the New Said; the Old Said had gone away.

I will now interpret some aspects of this vision: The journey is our life, a journey from the World of Spirits to all eternity, passing through the stages of the mother's womb, youth, old age, the grave, the Intermediate World, Resurrection, and the Bridge. The sixty gold coins are the sixty years of an average lifetime. I was forty-five when I had this vision. Only God knows when I will die. A sincere student of the Qur'an showed me the true path so that I might spend half of the remaining fifteen years for the Hereafter. The inn, I came to understand, was Istanbul for me. The train was time, and each wagon was a year. The tunnel was this worldly life. The thorny flowers and fruits were illicit pleasures and forbidden amusements that make the heart bleed with the idea of separation at the very moment you reach for them. Disappearance of pleasures increases sorrow, and besides, being unlawful, cause one to suffer punishment. The attendant had said: "Give me five cents, and I'll give you as many flowers and fruits as you want." This means that the permissible tastes and pleasures, obtained in lawful ways, are enough to satisfy us and so there is no need to pursue illicit ways.

FOURTH REMARK: Humanity, among the creatures, is much like a tender child. Our strength is in our weakness, and our power in our impotence. This lack of strength and power has caused creation to be subjugated to us. So if we perceive our weakness and become humble servants of God through verbal and active prayer, and if we recognize our impotence and seek God's help, we will have shown our gratitude to Him for this subjugation of nature to us. Moreover, God will enable us to reach our goal and achieve our aims in a way far beyond our own capability. Sometimes we wrongly attribute a wish's attainment to our own power and ability, when in reality it has been obtained for us through the prayer offered by the tongue of our disposition. Consider how great a source of power is a chick's weakness, for it causes the mother hen to attack even a lion. A lion cub's weakness subjugates a great lioness, which will suffer hunger to feed its baby. How remarkable is the powerful appeal inherent in weakness, and what a spectacular manifestation of Compassion for importunate beings.

Tender, beloved children obtain their goals by weeping, wishing, or making sad faces, all of which can cause mighty people to serve them. If children rely on their own strength, in practical terms they can achieve nothing. Their weakness and powerlessness, as well as feelings of affection and protection, are so in their favor that a single gesture may allow them to subjugate powerful persons to themselves. Should such children arrogantly deny the care and affection shown to them and claim to do all of this on their own, they would receive a sour face and resentment. Similarly, if like Korah who said: *I have been given it (my possessions) on account of my knowledge* (28:78), we attribute our achievements to our own power and ability in a way that demonstrates ingratitude and denies our Creator's Mercy and accuses His Wisdom, we will certainly deserve punishment.

This shows that our observed dominion in nature, and our advancement and progress in civilization and technology, are mainly due to our essential weakness and helplessness, which attract Divine aid. Our poverty is the source of Divine provision, our ignorance is compensated for by Divine inspiration, and our need draws Divine favors. Divine Mercy, Affection, and Wisdom, not our own power and knowledge, have empowered us with dominion over creation and have put things at our disposal. It is Divine Authority and Mercy Which, due to our weakness, enable us, beings so weak that we can be defeated by a blind scorpion and a footless snake, to dress in silk produced by a worm and to eat the honey produced by a stinging insect.

Since this is the reality, O humanity, renounce arrogance and self-trust. Rather, declare and affirm your impotence and weakness in God's Court by asking for His help, and by praying and entreating Him. Show that you are His true servant. Then say: *God is sufficient for us. How excellent a Guardian He is!* (3:173) and ascend to the higher ranks.

Do not say: "I am nothing. Why should the absolutely All-Wise One put creation at my disposal and demand universal gratitude?" In physical terms and with respect to your evil-commanding soul you are almost nothing, but your duty or rank makes you an attentive observer of this magnificent universe, an eloquent tongue of beings declaring Divine Wisdom, a perceptive student of this Book of Creation, an admiring overseer of the creatures glorifying God's praise, a respected master of worshipping beings.

You are, O humanity, an insignificant atom, a poor creature and weak animal in terms of your physical being and soul. And so you are being carried away by creation's huge waves. But if you are perfected through the training of Islam, which is illumined by the light of belief containing the radiance of Divine love, you will find a kingliness in your being a servant, a comprehensiveness in your particularity, a world in your small entity, and a very high rank in your insignificance. The realm of your supervision of the rest of creation will be so broad that you can say: "My Compassionate Lord has made the world a home for me. He has given me the sun and moon as lamps, spring as a bunch of roses, summer as a banquet of favors, and animals as obedient servants. He has put plants and vegetation at my disposal, as ornaments and provisions to my home."

In conclusion, if you obey your evil-commanding soul and Satan, you will fall to the lowest of the low; but if you follow the truth and the Qur'an, you will rise to the highest of the high and become the perfect pattern of creation.

FIFTH REMARK: We have been sent here as guests with a special responsibility. Endowed with important potentials, we have been assigned important duties and strongly urged to carry them out. If we do not, we will be punished. To make "being the perfect pattern of creation" more comprehensible, I will summarize the essentials of worship and duties.

Our worship has two aspects. The first aspect concerns reflection and consciousness without having to address Him directly. The second aspect is worship and prayer, done in His presence by addressing Him directly.

The first aspect is:

- to obediently affirm the Sovereignty of His Lordship over creation and observe Its beauties and perfections in amazement;

- to draw the attention to and herald the unique arts in creation, which consist of the embroideries of sacred Divine Names; to weigh on the scales of perception and discernment the gems of the Lord's Names, each of which is a hidden spiritual treasure, and evaluate them with our hearts' grateful appreciation;

- to study the pages of creation and the sheets of the heavens and the earth, each of which is a missive of Divine Power, and contemplate them in great admiration; and

- to gaze in amazement and admiration upon the subtle ornamentation and refined skills seen in creation, and ardently desire to know their All-Beautiful and Gracious Originator and yearn to enter His Presence, where we hope to be received into His favor.

The second aspect of our worship is done in His presence by addressing Him directly. We pass from the works to their Producer and:

- we see that an All-Majestic Maker wills Himself to be known through His Art's miracles, and in response we believe in Him and know Him;

- we see that an All-Compassionate Lord wills to make Himself loved through His Compassion's beautiful fruits, and in response we love Him and make ourselves loved by Him through devoting our love and adoration to Him;

- we see that an All-Munificent Provider nourishes us with the best and dearest of His material and spiritual favors, and we respond with gratitude and praise, expressed through our works, deeds, lifestyle and, if possible, through all of our senses and faculties;

- we see that an All-Beautiful and Gracious One of Majesty manifests His Grandeur and Perfection, Majesty and Beauty, in the mirrors of beings and draws attention to them, and in response, declaring, "God is the All-Great! All-Glorified is God!" we prostrate before Him in wonder and adoration, and in consciousness of our nothingness before Him;

- we see that One with Absolute Riches displays His limitless wealth and treasuries in an infinitely generous fashion, and, declaring our destitution, we respond with asking for His favors in praise and glorification;

- we see that that Originator of Majesty has arranged the earth like an exhibition to display His matchless works, and in response we appreciate them by saying, "What wonders God has willed and created!"; confirm their beauty by saying, "God bless them!"; show our wonder by saying: "All-Glorified is God!" and express our admiration by saying, "God is the All-Great!";

- we see that One absolutely Unique shows His Oneness throughout creation by His unique signs and specific decrees, and by His inimitable stamps and seals that He has put on each creature; that He inscribes signs of Unity on everything and raises throughout the world the flag of His Unity, proclaiming His Lordship. We respond to this with belief, affirmation, admission, and testimony to His Unity, and with devotion and sincere worship.

We may attain true humanity through such types of worship and reflection. We may show that we are of the best stature as the perfect pattern of creation and, by the grace of belief, become trustworthy rulers of the earth worthy of bearing the Supreme Trust.

Now, O heedless people who move toward the lowest of the low by misusing your will, although you have been created of the best stature as the perfect pattern of creation, listen to me. Like you, I once thought the world was fine and beautiful in heedlessness coming from the intoxication of youth. Then the moment I awoke in the morning of old age, I saw how ugly is the world's face which is not turned toward the Hereafter, which I had previously imagined to be beautiful. To see this and how extraordinarily beautiful is its other face, which is turned toward the Hereafter, you may refer to the two "Tables of Truth" in the Second Station of the Seventeenth Word.

The First Table depicts the reality of the world of the heedless, while the second one describes the reality of the world of the people of right guidance.

> All-Glorified are You! We have no knowledge save what You have taught us. Surely You are the All-Knowing, the All-Wise.

> O my Lord, expand for me my breast, and make my task easy for me. Loose any knot from my tongue so they may understand my speech.

> O God, bestow peace and blessings on Muhammad, his pure, unique essence, who is the sun of the heavens of mysteries, the manifestation of lights, the point upon which manifestations of God's Majesty are centered, the pivot around which the world of His Grace and Beauty revolves.

> O God, for the mystery of him in his relation to You, and for his journeying toward You, secure me from my fears, protect me from falling, diminish my faults, and expel my grief and greed. Be with me, take me away from myself unto You, and favor me with effacement from myself. Do not leave me obsessed with my self, veiled by my feelings. Unveil to me every mystery.

> O the All-Living and the Self-Subsisting, O the All-Living and the Self-Subsisting, O the All-Living and the Self-Subsisting! Have mercy upon me and my companions. Have mercy upon all believers and all the people of the Qur'an. Amin, O the Most Merciful of the Merciful, O the Most Munificent of the Munificent!

> The conclusion of their call will be: "All praise and gratitude are for God, the Lord of the worlds."

The Twenty-fourth Word

Love, worship and thanksgiving

In the Name of God, the All-Merciful, the All-Compassionate.

The fifth branch

HIS FIFTH BRANCH HAS FIVE FRUITS:

FIRST FRUIT: O MY SELFISH SOUL! O WORLDLY FRIEND! LOVE IS THE cause of the universe's existence, the bond between all things, and the light and life of the universe. Since we are the most comprehensive fruit of existence, a love so overflowing that it can invade the universe has been included in that fruit's heart (its seed or core). One who deserves such an infinite love can only be one with infinite perfection.

Therefore, O soul and friend, our nature contains two faculties: the means of fear and the means of love. Such love and fear is felt for either the created or the Creator. Fear of the created is a painful affliction, and love of the created is a troublesome pain, for you fear such things or persons that they show you no mercy or reject your request. If this is so, fear of the created is a painful affliction. As for love of the created, those you love either do not care for you and, like your youth and possessions, leave you without saying farewell. Or they disdain you because of your love. Ninety-nine percent of lovers complain of their beloved ones, for love of the idol-like worldly beloved from the bottom of one's heart, which is the mirror of the Eternally Besought One, is unbearable in the beloved's view. And so it is rejected, for human nature rejects and repels what is unnatural and undeserved. (Animal love is out of question here.)

In short, those you love either do not care for you, or they despise you, or they do not accompany you. Contrary to your desire, they leave you. So turn your fear and love toward such a One that your fear will be a pleasant humility and your love a happiness free of humiliation. Fearing the All-Majestic Creator means finding a way to His Compassion and taking refuge in Him. In fact, fear is a whip; it drives one into the embrace of His Compassion. A mother frightens her child away from something or someone and attracts him into her arms. That fear is very pleasurable for children, for it draws them into the arms of care and compassion. However, the care and compassion of all mothers is only a ray from His Compassion. This means there is a great pleasure in fear of God. Given this, you can understand what infinite pleasure can be found by loving Him. Furthermore, those who fear God are freed from the worrying, troublesome fear of others, and their love of created beings in God's Name causes no pain or separation.

We, first of all, love our own selves, and then our families and relatives, then our nation, then living beings, then the world or the universe. We have relations with all of these spheres, feel pleasure in their satisfaction and happiness, and pain at their pain. But since everything is impermanent in this tumultuous and ever-changing world, our heart is wounded continuously. What we cling to slips out of our hands, scratching and cutting them on the way. We remain in pain or throw ourselves into the drunkenness of heedlessness.

Since this is so, O soul, if you have sense, give all the love you divide among beings to the One Who truly deserves it and thereby save yourself from all pain and trouble. Only One Who owns infinite perfection and beauty deserves infinite love. Only when you can assign that love to its rightful owner can you love, for His sake and in respect of their being mirrors to Him, all things without pain or trouble. Such love must not be assigned directly to existence for the sake of existence itself. Otherwise, while being a most pleasurable Divine grace, love becomes a most painful ailment.

Another, more important, aspect of the matter, my soul, is that you assign your love to your self. You idolize your self and see it as worthy of adoration. You sacrifice everything for your self and revere it as though it were the Lord. However, something is loved either for its perfection (which is loved because of itself), or for the benefit or pleasure it gives, the good it brings, or for another, similar reason. Now, O soul! I have presented convincing arguments in some of the Words that your nature is "kneaded together" out of defect and deficiency, as well as destitution and impotence. As darkness shows light's strength in proportion to its density, by way of contrast, you are a mirror through those essential elements of your nature to the All-Majestic Originator's Perfection, Grace, Beauty, Power, and Mercy.

So, O soul, you should cherish enmity for your self or have pity on it. Or you should treat it with care and mercy after it has full conviction of the truth of the principles of belief and satisfaction in worship.

If you love your (carnal) self, which is addicted to pleasure and always looks after its own interest, you have been captivated by pleasure and self-interest. Do not prefer such insignificant pleasure and self-interest over boundless true pleasure and advantage. Do not be like a firefly, which drowns its friends and everything it loves in the fright and solitude of darkness and contents itself with its own tiny glow. Love the Eternally Beloved One in Whose favor originate, along with your animal pleasures and interests, the interests of all beings with whom you have relations, from whom you receive benefit, and whose happiness makes you happy. This will enable you to take pleasure in their happiness and to receive the same infinite pleasure as you receive from the Absolutely Perfect One.

Your intense self-love is in fact nothing but your innate love for His "Essence," which you unconsciously carry in yourself and wrongly appropriate for your self. Tear apart the "I" in yourself and show the "He." All the love you divide among other beings is nothing but the love implanted in your being for His Names and Attributes. But you misuse it and so suffer pain and trouble, for the return of an illicit love cherished for those who are unworthy of it is pitiless ailment.

An atom of love for the Eternal, Beloved One, Who through His Names the All-Merciful and All-Compassionate has created a Paradise full of *houris* to satisfy all your bodily desires, Who through His other Names has prepared there for you eternal favors to meet all the needs of your immaterial faculties (e.g., your spirit, heart, intellect, and innermost senses), and in each of Whose Names are numerous immaterial treasuries of favor and munificence, may compensate for the universe. However, the universe cannot compensate for even one particular manifestation of His love. Given this, listen and obey the following eternal decree, which the Eternal, Beloved One made His beloved, His Messenger, declare: *If you really love God, follow me [so] that God may love you* (3:31).

SECOND FRUIT: O soul! Worship of God is not an act through which to demand a Divine reward in the future, but rather the necessary result of a past Divine favor. We have received our wages and, in return, are charged with serving and worshipping Him. For, O soul, the All-Majestic Creator Who clothed you in existence, which is purely good, has given you a hungry stomach and, through His Name the All-Providing, has laid before you all edible things as a table of favors. Also, He has given you a life decked out with senses. It too demands its own particular sustenance like a stomach. All your senses like eyes and ears are like hands before which He has laid a particular table of favors as vast as the earth. In addition, as He has made you human, which demands numerous immaterial favors, He has laid before you a table of favors within reason's grasp and as multidimensional as the material and immaterial worlds. As He has also granted you belief and Islam, which is the greatest humanity and thus demands endless favors and is nourished by the fruits of infinite Mercy, He has opened up for you a table of favors, happiness, and pleasures which encompasses, together with the Sphere of Contingencies, the Sphere of His All-Beautiful Names and sacred Attributes. Moreover, by bestowed on you love, which is a light of belief, He has granted to you still another table of favors, bliss, and pleasures.

In physical terms you are a small, insignificant, impotent, wretched, and restricted particular being. But through His grace and favors you have become a universal, enlightened, and enlightening being. He has endowed you with life and thereby promoted you to the rank of a particular kind of universality. By endowing you with humanity, He has raised you to the rank of true universality, and by granting to you Islam, to the the rank of a sublime and luminous universality; and by bestowing on you love and knowledge of God, He has made you attain an all-encompassing light.

O soul! As you have received these wages already, you are charged with worship, which is an easy, pleasant, and rewarding Divine gift. But you are lazy when it comes to performing it. When you carry it out defectively, as though you consider the advance wages insufficient, you arrogantly demand more. You also put on airs and complain that your prayers are not accepted. Your due is not complaint but offering petitions and supplications to God Almighty. He bestows Paradise and eternal happiness purely out of His Grace and Kindness. Therefore, always seek refugee in His Mercy and Grace, rely on Him, and heed the following Divine declaration: *Say: "Out of His Grace and Mercy," and at that let them rejoice. It is better than what they have been accumulating* (10:58).

If you ask: "How can I respond to those universal, infinite favors through my restricted, particular thankfulness?", the answer will what follows: Through a universal intention and infinitely profound belief and devotion. Suppose a poor man enters the king's presence with a cheap (in materialistic terms) present. There he sees expensive gifts sent by the king's favorites. He thinks: "My present means nothing, but this is what I can afford." Then suddenly he addresses the king, saying: "My lord! I offer all these precious gifts in my name, for you deserve them. If I could, I would offer a double of these."

The king, who needs nothing but accepts his subjects' gifts as tokens of respect and loyalty, accepts the poor man's universal intention, desire, and deep feelings of devotion as though they were the greatest gift. Similarly, a poor servant says in his daily Prescribed Prayers: "All worship and veneration is for God," by which he means: "In my name, I offer You all the gifts of worship that all beings present to you through their lives. You deserve all of them, and in reality far more than them." This belief and intention is a most comprehensive and universal thankfulness.

The seeds and stones of plants are their intentions to grow into elaborate plants. For example, with its hundreds of seeds, a melon intends: "O my Creator! I want to exhibit the inscriptions of Your All-Beautiful Names in many places of the earth." Having full knowledge of the future, Almighty God accepts its intentions as worship in deeds. The Prophetic saying: "A believer's intention is better than his action,"[15] expresses this reality. This is also why we glorify and praise Him with phrases expressing infinitude, like: "Glory be to You, and praise be to You to the number of Your creatures, the things pleasing to You, the decorations of Your Supreme Throne, to the amount of the ink of Your words. We glorify You with the sum of all the glorifications of Your Prophets, saints, and angels."

Just as a commander offers the king, in his name, all of his soldiers' services, humanity, the commander of all earthly creatures (including plants and animals) and acting in its own private world as if in the name of everyone, says: *You alone do we worship and from You alone do we seek help* (1:5), and offers the All-Worshipped One of Majesty in humanity's name all of

---

[15] al-Munawi, *Faydu'l-Qadir*, 6:291.

the creation's worship and entreaties for help. Saying: "Glory be to You with the sum of all the glorifications of all Your creatures and with the tongues of all things You have made," humanity makes all creatures speak in its own name.

Also, humanity says: "O God! Bestow blessings on Muhammad to the number of atoms and compounds in the universe." He calls God's blessing on Prophet Muhammad in the name of everything, for everything is connected with the light of Muhammad, upon him be peace and blessings. Understand from all this the wisdom in glorifying God and calling His blessings on Muhammad to the extent of infinity.

THIRD FRUIT: O soul! If you want endless accomplishments with regard to your afterlife during your short life here, if you want to see each minute of your life as fruitful as a whole life, and if you want to transform your ordinary deeds into acts of worship and your heedlessness into constant awareness of being in God's Presence, follow the Prophet's exalted Sunna. For obeying the rules of the Shari'a affords some sort of awareness of God's presence, and becomes a kind of worship that yields many fruits for the Hereafter.

For example, when you follow the principle which the Shari'a requires in a buy-and-sell transaction, this ordinary transaction becomes an act of worship, for remembering the Shari'a reminds you of the Divine Revelation, which causes you to think of the Revealer of the Shari'a and to turn your attention to Him. This produces awareness of His presence. That means, obeying the Sunna can make one's transient life produce eternal fruits to be the means of an eternal life. Therefore, heed the following Divine decree: *So believe in God and His Messenger, the unlettered Prophet who believes in God and His words, and follow him so that you may be guided* (7:158). Try to be a comprehensive object to be enlightened by each Divine Beautiful Name manifested in the rules of the Shari'a and the exalted Sunna.

FOURTH FRUIT: O soul! Do not be deluded by the apparent glitter and illicit pleasure of worldly people, particularly of those leading a dissolute life and, even more particularly, unbelievers. For you will not able to be like them by imitating them. You will fall too low. You cannot be like animals either, for your intellect will be an inauspicious "tool" that will give you endless trouble.

Suppose there is a palace the central room of which has a large electric light. All other rooms have small lights connected to it. If someone turns off that large light, the palace is left in darkness. Another palace has small electric lights in each room that are not connected to its central light. If that palace owner turns off the central light, the other rooms remain illuminated. This allows its inhabitants to do their work and deter thieves.

O soul! The first palace represents Muslims. Our Prophet, upon him be peace and blessings, is the large central light in the Muslims' heart. If they forget him or discard him from their heart, they will be unable to believe in any other Prophet. Moreover, their spirit will have no room for any kind of perfection. They will not recognize their Lord, all their inner senses and faculties will be left in darkness, and their hearts will be ruined and invaded by despair and gloom. What will be able to find to replace the resulting void with and find consolation in?

Christians and Jews are like the other palace. Even if they are not illuminated by the Prophet's light, they can manage with the "light" they think they have. Their form of belief in the Creator and Moses or Jesus, upon them be peace, can still be the means of some sort of moral perfection.

O evil-commanding soul! You can never be like an animal either, for your intellect troubles you continuously with pains of the past and anxieties for the future. It blends one pleasure with a thousand pains. But an animal enjoys itself without pain. So if you want to live like an animal, first discard your intellect and then be an animal. Also, be attentive to the Divine warning: *They are like cattle, rather, more astray (and in need of being led)* (7:179).

FIFTH FRUIT: O soul! Since we are the fruit of the Tree of Creation, we are a most comprehensive being and are related to all creation. We have within ourselves a heart that, like a fruit's pit, is the center in which all parts end and join together. We are mortal and inclined toward the world of multiplicity. But the worship of God is a line of union that turns us from mortality toward permanence, from the created toward the Creator, and from multiplicity toward unity. It is also a point of juncture between the beginning and the end.

If a seed-bearing fruit looks down at those under the tree and, priding itself on its beauty, throws itself into their hands or heedlessly leaps off the tree, it is quickly lost. However, if it is not heedless of its point of support, its seed (in which the tree's whole life is included) will enable the tree to perpetuate its meaning and life. This also enables it to gain a comprehensive reality in a perpetual life.

Similarly, if you are drowned in the multiplicity of things and, deluded with the smiles of mortals in drunkenness with love of the world, leave yourself in their arms, you will certainly suffer utter loss and find yourself in the darkness of eternal execution after a transient life. This will also bring about your spiritual death. But if you listen to the lessons of belief from the Qur'an with the ear of your heart and coming to your senses, turn toward unity, you will be able to reach the summit of perfections through worship and servanthood to God, and gain eternal existence.

O soul! Since this is the reality and since you are from Abraham's nation, say, like he did: "I love not those that set." Turn your face toward the Eternal Beloved One, and weep saying the following lines.

(The verses to be included here have been included in the Second Station of the Seventeenth Word, and have not been repeated here.)

The Twenty-fifth Word

The miracaluousness or inimitability of the Qur'an

In the Name of God, the All-Merciful, the All-Compassionate.

The second radiance of the third ray:
The Qur'an's ever-freshness

THIS RELATES TO THE QUR'AN'S FRESHNESS, WHICH IS MAINTAINED AS if it were revealed anew in every epoch. As an eternal discourse addressing all human beings regardless of time or place and level of understanding, it should—and does—have a never-fading freshness.

The Qur'an so impresses each new generation that each one regards it as being revealed to itself and receives its instructions therefrom. Human words and laws become old and so need to be revised or changed. But the Qur'an's laws and principles are so established and constant, so compatible with essential human nature and creation's unchanging laws, that the passage of time has no effect upon them. Instead, it shows the Qur'an's truth, validity, and force even more clearly! Especially the people of this twentieth century, including particularly its People of the Book,[16] who rely on themselves more than any preceding people's self-reliance and close their ears to the Qur'an's calls, are most in need of the Qur'anic calls of guidance beginning with: *O People of the Book!* As this phrase also means "O people of schooling and education," it is as if those messages were directed toward this century exclusively. With all its strength and freshness, the Qur'an makes the whole world resound with its call: Say: "*O People of the Book! Come to a word common between us and you, that we worship none but God, and that we associate none as partner with Him, and that none of us take others for Lords, apart from God.*" (3:64)

---

16 Jews and Christians (Tr.)

Modern civilization, the product of human ideas and perhaps of the jinn, has chosen to contend with the Qur'an, which no one has ever been able to do. It tries to contradict its miraculousness through its charm and "spells." To prove the Qur'an's miraculousness or inimitability against this new, terrible opponent, and affirm its challenge of: *Say: "If humanity and jinn banded together to produce the like of this Qur'an, they would never produce its like, even though they backed one another"* (17:88), I will compare modern civilization's basic principles and foundations with those of the Qur'an.

First, all of the comparisons and criteria put forward from The First Word to this Twenty-fifth One, and the truths and verses contained therein and upon which they are based, prove the Qur'an's miraculousness and indisputable superiority over modern civilization.

Second, as convincingly argued in The Twelfth Word: By reason of its philosophy, modern civilization considers force or might to be the point of support in social life, and the realization of self-interest is its goal. It holds that the principle of life is conflict. The unifying bonds between the members of a community and communities are race and aggressive nationalism; and its ultimate aim is the gratification of carnal desires and the continuous increase of human needs. However, force calls for aggression, seeking self-interest causes fighting over material resources, which do not suffice for the satisfaction of all desires; and conflict brings strife. Racism feeds by swallowing others, thereby paving the way for aggression. It is because of these principles of modern civilization that despite all its positive aspects, it has been able to provide some sort of superficial happiness for only twenty per cent of humanity and cast eighty per cent into distress and poverty.

As for the Qur'anic wisdom, it accepts right, not might, as the point of support in social life. Its goal is virtue and God's approval, not the realization of self-interests. Its principle of life is mutual assistance, not conflict. The only community bonds it accepts are those of religion, profession, and country. Its final aims are controlling carnal desires and urging the soul to sublime matters, satisfying our exalted feelings so that we will strive for human perfection and true humanity. Right calls for unity, virtues bring solidarity, and mutual assistance means hastening to help one another. Religion secures brotherhood, sisterhood, and cohesion. Restraining our carnal soul and desires and urging the soul to perfection brings happiness in this world and the next.

Thus despite its borrowings from previous Divine religions and especially the Qur'an, which accounts for its agreeable aspects, modern civilization cannot offer a viable alternative to the Qur'an.

Third, I will give a few examples of the Qur'an's many subjects and commandments. As its laws and principles transcend time and space, they do not become obsolete; they are always fresh and strong. For example, despite all its charitable foundations, institutions of intellectual and moral training, and severe disciplines and laws and regulations, modern civilization has been unable to contest the wise Qur'an even on the following two matters and has been defeated by it:

First comparison: Perform the Prescribed Prayer, and pay the Zakah (2:43); and: *God has made trading lawful and interest and usury unlawful* (2:275). As explained in my *Isharatu'l-I'jaz* (Signs of the Qur'an's Miraculousness), as the origin of all revolutions and corruption is one phrase, so is the cause and source of all vices and moral failings also one phrase: The first is: "I am full, so what is it to me if others die of hunger?" And the second: "You work so that I may eat."

A peaceful social life depends on the balance between the elite (rich) and common (poor) people. This balance is based on the former's care and compassion and the latter's respect and compliance. Ignoring the first attitude drives the rich to wrongdoing, usurpation, immorality, and mercilessness; ignoring the second attitude drives the poor to hatred, grudges, envy, and conflict with the rich. As this conflict has destroyed social peace for the last two or three centuries, it has also caused social upheavals in Europe due to the struggle between labor and capital.

Despite all its charitable societies, institutions of moral training, and severe laws and regulations, modern civilization has neither reconciled these two social classes nor healed those two severe wounds of human life. The Qur'an, however, eradicates the first attitude and heals its wounds through the *Zakah*, and eradicates the second by outlawing interest and usury. The abovementioned Qur'anic verse stands at the door of the world and says to interest and usury: "You are forbidden to enter!" It decrees to humanity, "If you want to close the door of strife, close the door of interest and usury," and orders its students not to enter through it.

Second comparison: Modern civilization rejects polygamy as unwise and disadvantageous to social life. Indeed, even though the purpose of marriage were sexual gratification, polygamy would be a lawful way to realize it. But as observed even in animals and plants, the basic purpose for and wisdom in sexual relations is reproduction. The resulting pleasure is a small payment determined by Divine Mercy to realize this duty. Thus, as marriage is for reproduction and perpetuation of the species, being able to give birth at most once a year, to be impregnated only during half of a month, and entering menopause around fifty, one woman is usually insufficient for a man, who can sometimes impregnate even until the age of a hundred. That is why, in most cases, modern civilization has been compelled to tolerate numerous houses of prostitution.

Third comparison: Modern civilization criticizes the wise Qur'an for giving a woman one-third of the inheritance (half of her brother's share) while giving a man two-thirds. However, general circumstances are considered when establishing general rules and laws. In this case, a woman usually finds a man to maintain her, whereas a man usually has to live with one of whom he must take care. Given this, a woman's husband is to make up the difference between her share of the inheritance and that of her brother. Her brother, on the other hand, will spend half of his inheritance on his wife [and children], equaling his sister's share. This is true justice.

Fourth comparison: The Qur'an severely prohibits idolatry and condemns the adoration of images, which can be an imitation of idolatry. However, modern civilization sees sculpture and the portrayal of living beings, which the Qur'an condemns, as one of its virtues. Forms with or without shadows (sculptures and pictures of living beings) are either a petrified tyranny (tyranny represented in stone), embodied ostentation or solidified passion, all of which excite lust and urge people to tyranny, ostentation, and capriciousness.

Out of compassion, the Qur'an orders women to wear the veil of modesty to maintain respect for them and to prevent their transformation into objects of low desire or being used to excite lust. Modern civilization, however, has drawn women out of their homes, torn aside their veils, and led humanity into corruption. Family life is based on mutual love and respect between men and women, but immodest dress has destroyed sincere love and respect, and poisoned family life. Sculptures and pictures, especially obscene ones, have a great share in this moral corruption and spiritual degeneration. Just as looking at the corpse of a beautiful woman who deserves compassion with lust and desire destroys morality, looking lustfully at pictures of living women, which are like little corpses, troubles and diverts, shakes and destroys elevated human feelings.

In conclusion, then, besides securing happiness for all people in this world, the Qur'anic commandments serve their eternal happiness. You can compare other matters with those mentioned.

Just as modern civilization stands defeated before the Qur'an's rules and principles for social life and humanity, and bankrupt before the Qur'an's miraculous content, so also the Words written so far, primarily the Eleventh and Twelfth, demonstrate that European philosophy and scientism, the spirit of that civilization, are helpless when confronted with the Qur'an's wisdom. In addition, when compared to the Qur'an's literary merits—which may be likened to an elevated lover's uplifting songs arising from temporary separation or heroic epics encouraging its audience to victory and lofty sacrifices—modern civilization's literature and rhetoric appear as an orphan's desperate, grief-stricken wailing or a drunkard's noise.

Styles of literature and rhetoric give rise to sorrow or joy. Sorrow is of two kinds: it comes from either the feeling of loneliness and lack of any protection and support, or separation from the beloved. The first is despairing and produced by modern misguided naturalist, and heedless civilization. The second is lofty and exhilarating, and arouses a hope and eagerness for reunion. This is the kind given by the guiding, light-diffusing Qur'an.

Joy also is of two kinds. The first incites the soul to animal desires (so-called "fine" arts, drama, and cinema, etc.). The second restrains the carnal soul and urges (in a mannerly, innocent way) the human heart, spirit, intellect, and all inner senses and faculties to lofty things and reunion with the original, eternal abode and with friends who have passed on already. The Qur'an of miraculous exposition encourages this joy by arousing an eagerness to reach Paradise, eternal happiness, and the vision of God Almighty.

Thus the profound meaning and great truth contained in: *Say: "If humanity and jinn banded together to produce the like of this Qur'an, they would never produce its like, even if they backed one another"* (17:88), is not, as some assert, an exaggeration. It is pure truth and reality, which the long history of Islam has proved. The challenge contained here has two principal aspects. One is that no human or jinn work can resemble or equal the Qur'an's style, eloquence, rhetoric, wording, comprehensiveness, conciseness, and profundity. Nor can their most beautiful and eloquent words, all arranged in a volume by their most competent representatives, equal the Qur'an. The second aspect is that all human and jinn civilizations, philosophies, literatures, and laws, which are the products of the thought and efforts of humanity and the jinn and even satans, are dim and helpless when faced with the Qur'an's commandments, wisdom, and eloquence.

The Eleventh Ray

Some of belief's fruits

In the Name of God, the All-Merciful, the All-Compassionate.

An addendum to the Tenth Matter:
Belief changes all gloom and loneliness into joy

FTER OUR RELEASE FROM DENIZLI PRISON, I WAS SITTING ON THE TOP floor of the well-known Hotel Şehir. The graceful dancing of the leaves, branches, and trunks of the poplar trees in the fine gardens opposite me, each with a rapturous motion like a circle of dervishes touched by the breeze, pained my heart, which was already grieving at being parted from my brothers and finding myself alone. Suddenly I thought of fall and winter, and a kind of heedlessness overcame me. I pitied those graceful, swaying poplars and joyful living creatures so much that my eyes began to brim with tears. Since they reminded me of the deaths and separations which lie beneath the ornamented veil of the cosmic façade, the grief at a world full of death and separation took me in its grip and began to squeeze me. But then the light of the *Truth of Muhammad* came and changed that grief to joy. Indeed, I felt eternally grateful to the person of Muhammad, upon him be peace and blessings, for the help and consolation that came to me at that time, for only a single instance of the boundless grace of that light for me, as for all believers and everyone. It was as follows:

The heedlessness that had overcome me had shown me that these blessed and delicate creatures only appear in the season of summer in a purposeless and fruitless life. Their movements were not due to joy; rather they were trembling at the thought of death, separation, and the journey to non-existence. This view was deeply injurious to my passionate desire for permanence, to my love of beauty and my compassion for all creatures and living things. This way of thinking transformed the world into a kind of Hell and my intellect into an instrument of torture. But just at that point, the light that Prophet Muhammad, upon him be peace and blessings, brought as a gift for humanity lifted the veil and showed that rather than extinction, non-existence, nothingness, futility, or separation, the existence of these poplar trees had as many meanings and purposes as the number of their leaves. Moreover, it revealed that they had several duties and that their lives yielded many results, as follows:

One kind relates to the All-Majestic Maker's Names. For example, everyone applauds and congratulates an engineer who makes an extraordinary machine. By carrying out its functions properly, the machine in turn can be said to congratulate and applaud its engineer. Every created being in the universe is such a machine and congratulates and applauds its Maker.

Another instance of wisdom in things such as poplar trees is that each of them resembles a text which, when studied, reveals knowledge of God to conscious living beings. Having left their meanings in the minds of beings such as these, and having left their forms in these beings' memories, as well as on the tablets of the World of representations or "ideal forms" and the records of the World of the Unseen, they leave the material world for the World of the Unseen. In other words, they are stripped of apparent existence and gain many existences that pertain to meanings, the Knowledge that lies behind them and the knowledge of conscious beings, and the unseen realm.

Since God exists and His Knowledge encompasses all things, certainly there can be no such thing in reality, or in the world of a believer, as non-existence, eternal annihilation, or nothingness. An unbeliever's world, however, is filled with notions such as non-existence, separation, and extinction. As the famous proverb has it: "Everything exists for the one for whom God exists; nothing exists for the one for whom God does not exist."

In short, then, just as belief saves us from eternal punishment when we die, it saves everyone's particular world from the darkness of eternal extinction and nothingness. Unbelief, especially the denial of God, destroys both the individual themselves and their particular world with the fear of death, casting them into dark, hellish pits and changing their life's pleasures into pain. Those who prefer this world over the Hereafter should pay heed to this. They should either find a solution for this intractable problem or they should accept belief, thus saving themselves from a most fearful eternal loss.

> All-Glorified are You! We have no knowledge save what You have taught us. Surely You are the All-Knowing, the All-Wise.

The Twenty-sixth Word

Belief in Divine Destiny and silencing the obstinate, arrogant soul

In the Name of God, the All-Merciful, the All-Compassionate.

 QUESTION: IF WE ARE BOUND BY DIVINE DESTINY TO CERTAIN EXTENTS though it considers our free will as well, is belief in Destiny not a burden for the heart and spirit, which are so desirous of free activity and self-perfection?

ANSWER: Absolutely not! Rather, it provides the spirit with relief, security, and comfort. If we do not believe in Destiny, the spirit has to endure a burden as heavy as the earth for the sake of an illusory, temporary, and very limited freedom. For we are connected with the whole universe, and cherish limitless desires and ambitions, none of which we can satisfy on our own. Eventually, we will be left alone with insupportable trouble and torment. Belief in Destiny places this burden on the vessel of Destiny, and allows the heart and spirit to work for their perfection with perfect ease and freedom. It only takes away the carnal soul's illusory freedom and breaks its tyrannical hold over us. Belief in Destiny gives us a pleasure and happiness beyond description.

Consider this comparison: Two people enter a splendid palace. One does not recognize the king and tries to live there on theft and usurpation. However, he finds it hard to control the palace and its inhabitants, take care of the garden, carry out the king's affairs with the necessary calculation and management, operate the machines, and feed the animals. As a result, this "paradise" turns into "hell" for him. Finally, he is imprisoned because of his defective management and corruption. The other person recognizes the king and is aware of being his guest. He perceives and believes that the affairs of the palace and the garden are carried out under the king's rule and authority. Understanding that the king assumes full responsibility for governing the palace, he enjoys the pleasures of living there and does not interfere. He overlooks certain things that appear disagreeable, trusting in the king's compassion and his administration's justice and wisdom. As a result, he lives a contented and pleasant life. Reflect on this comparison and understand the adage: Whoever believes in Destiny is free from anxiety.

Fourth topic

QUESTION: The First Topic proves that whatever is determined by Destiny is good, that even apparently evil deeds are actually good, and that ugly things are essentially beautiful. But do the calamities and tribulations suffered in this world not contradict this?

ANSWER: O my carnal soul and my friend, you feel agony because of your strong connections with existence and affection toward beings. Existence is entirely good, for it generates every beauty and perfection; non-existence [which absorbs every good like black holes] is purely evil, for all sin and misfortune originate in it. Given this, whatever contains a hint of non-existence contains an element of evil. So, life, the most brilliant light of existence, becomes stronger as it is confronted with different circumstances. It is purified and perfected through contradictory events and happenings, and produces the desired results by assuming different qualities. Thus it testifies to the impresses of Names of the Giver of life. It is because of this subtle reality that living creatures pass through many states and experience pains, tribulations and hardship, through which the lights of existence are continuously renewed in their lives, and the darkness of non-existence draws distant and their lives are purified. In quality and as conditions, idleness, inertia, and monotony are aspects of non-existence. Monotony reduces even the greatest pleasure to nothing.

In short, since life displays the impresses of God's All-Beautiful Names, everything occurring in it is beautiful. Consider this: A very rich and infinitely skilled clothes designer uses an ordinary model to display his works of art in return for wages. He requires the model to dress in a jeweled and artistically fashioned garment that illustrates his work's art and his invaluable wealth. He continues to modify the garment while the model wears it. Does the model have any right to say: "Your orders to bow and stand up are causing me trouble. Your cutting and shortening of this garment, which makes me more beautiful, spoils my beauty." Can the model accuse the designer of treating him unkindly and unfairly?

Similarly, in order to display the impresses of His All-Beautiful Names, the Maker of Majesty, the peerless All-Originating, alters within numerous circumstances the garment of existence He clothes on living creatures, bejeweled with senses, reason, intellect, and heart. Circumstances that appear to be calamitous and painful are actually rays of Divine Mercy within gleams of Wisdom and contain subtle beauties. They show the acts and impresses of the Divine All-Beautiful Names.

Conclusion

This consists of Four Paragraphs which silenced the Old Said's obstinate, proud, and conceited soul, and compelled it to submit.

FIRST PARAGRAPH: Since things exist and have been made with skill, a Supreme Maker must exist. If everything's existence is not ascribed to One Being, the existence of a single thing would become as difficult as the existence of all things. But if everything is ascribed to One Being, the creation of all things becomes as easy as the creation of one thing. Since One Being has created the earth and the heavens, for sure that All-Wise and Skillful Creator would not allow disorder to arise by allowing others to create and administer living beings, who are the fruits and aims of the heavens and the earth, and so He would not mock His Divine purpose for creation. He would certainly not give others their worship and thanks.

SECOND PARAGRAPH: O my haughty carnal soul! You are like a grapevine. The vine itself has not attached the bunches of grapes; someone else has attached them, so do not boast.

THIRD PARAGRAPH: O my ostentatious carnal soul! Do not be proud of your services to God's religion. As stated in a Prophetic Tradition, God may strengthen this religion by means of a dissolute person. You are not pure, so regard yourself as that dissolute person. Purge yourself of self-admiration and pride by considering your service and worship as thanksgiving for God's past favors to you, a duty required by your humanity and a consequence of your being God's work of art.

FOURTH PARAGRAPH: If you want to acquire knowledge of the truth and true wisdom, try to attain knowledge of God. For all truths and realities of creation consist in the rays of the Divine Name of the Ultimate Truth and Ever-Constant and the manifestations of His Names and Attributes.

The reality of each human being and every existence, whether material or spiritual, substantial or accidental, originates in the light of one of His Names. Otherwise they would be mere forms without any substantial reality and truth.

O my carnal soul! If you are attached to this temporary worldly life and try to flee from death, know that life is the present moment. The past and what existed therein have passed away, and the future and what will exist therein is still non-existent. Thus the material life upon which you rely is of momentary duration. Some truth-knowing scholars even say that life consists of an instant. For this reason, some saints believe that the world is non-existent on account of itself. As this is the reality, abandon the corporeal, carnal life and rise to the level of life of the heart, spirit, and innermost faculties. See what a broad sphere of life they have. The past and future, which are dead for you, are living for them; they are existent and full of life. Given this, O my carnal soul, shed tears like my heart, and cry out and say:

> I am mortal, so I do not want the mortal.
> I am impotent, so I do not desire the impotent.
> I surrendered my spirit to the All-Merciful, so I desire none else.
> I want only one who will remain my friend forever.
> I am but an insignificant particle, but I desire an everlasting sun.
> I am nothing in essence, but I wish for the whole of creation.

The Thirtieth Word

An exposition of ego or human selfhood

In the Name of God, the All-Merciful, the All-Compassionate.

We offered the Trust to the heavens, and the earth, and the mountains, but they shrank from bearing it, and were afraid of it (fearful of being unable to fulfill its responsibility), but humanity has undertaken it; humanity is indeed prone to doing great wrong and misjudging, and acting out of sheer ignorance. (33:72)

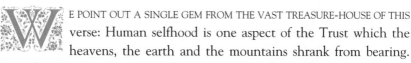E POINT OUT A SINGLE GEM FROM THE VAST TREASURE-HOUSE OF THIS verse: Human selfhood is one aspect of the Trust which the heavens, the earth and the mountains shrank from bearing. From the time of Adam up to the present, it has been the seed of the terrible tree of *Zaqqum* and of the illustrious tree of *Touba*, which have shot out branches around the world of humankind. Before shedding some light on this great truth, we offer the following introductory explanation.

Selfhood is the key to the Divine Names, which are hidden treasures. Being a mystery and a wonderful talisman, it also is the key to creation's mystery. When its essence is known, its mystery is resolved, and that, in turn, discloses creation's mystery and the Necessary Existence's treasuries. I discussed this in my Arabic treatise, *A Whiff from the Breezes of the Qur'an's Guidance* (included in *al-Mathnawi an-Nuri*), as follows:

The key to creation is in our hand and attached to our selfhood. The doors to creation seem to be open, but in fact are closed. The All-Mighty has entrusted us with a key (Ego or Selfhood) that will open creation's doors and reveal the hidden treasures of the Creator of the universe. However, Selfhood itself is a difficult mystery and an enigma, but if its true nature and purpose are known, both itself and creation's mystery will be solved.

The All-Wise Maker has entrusted each human being with selfhood having clues and samples to urge and enable him or her to recognize the truths about His Lordship's attributes and essential characteristics. Selfhood is the measure or means of comparison that makes Lordship's attributes and Divinity's characteristics known. A measure or means of comparison does not have to have actual existence, for its posited or supposed existence can serve as a measure, just like hypothetical lines in geometry.

QUESTION: Why did God make our selfhood a means to know His Attributes and Names?

ANSWER: An absolute and all-encompassing entity has no limits or terms, and therefore cannot be shaped or formed; neither can it be determined in such a way that its essential nature can be comprehended. For example, an endless light undetermined by darkness cannot be known or perceived. But whenever a real or hypothetical bounding line of darkness is drawn, it becomes determined and known. In the same way, the Divine Attributes and Names (e.g., Knowledge, Power, Wisdom, and Compassion) cannot be determined, for they are all-encompassing and have no limits or like. Thus what they essentially are cannot be known or perceived. A hypothetical boundary is needed for them to become known.

In our case, this hypothetical boundary is our selfhood. It imagines within itself a fictitious lordship, power, and knowledge, and so posits a bounding line, hypothesizes a limit to the all-encompassing Divine Attributes, and says: "This is mine, and the rest is His." Selfhood thus makes a division. By means of the miniature measures it contains, Selfhood slowly comes to understand the true nature of the Divine Attributes and Names.

For example, through this imagined lordship in its own sphere, Selfhood can understand the Lordship of the Creator in the universe. By means of its own apparent ownership, it can understand the real Ownership of its Creator, saying: "As I am the owner of this house, the Creator is the Owner of this universe." Through its partial knowledge, Selfhood comes to understand His Absolute Knowledge. Through its defective, acquired art, it can intuit the All-Majestic Maker's matchless, originative Art. It says: "I built and arranged this house, so there must be One Who made and arranged this universe."

Human ego or selfhood contains thousands of states, attributes, and perceptions that, to some extent, disclose and make knowable the Divine

Attributes and essential Characteristics. Like a mirror, a measure, an instrument for discovering, or a letter which has no meaning in itself but serves the word's meaning, Selfhood is a strand of consciousness from the thick rope of human existence, a fine thread from the celestial weave of humanity's essential nature, an *alif*[17] from the book of human identity and character.

That *alif* (I) has two aspects or faces. One aspect relates to good and existence and only receives passively what is given; it cannot create. The other aspect or face relates to evil and derives from non-existence. Here Selfhood is active. Its real nature is indicative—like a letter that has no meaning by or in itself—and points to the meaning of things other than itself. Its lordship is fictitious and hypothetical, and its own existence is so weak and insubstantial that it cannot bear or support anything on its own. Rather, Selfhood is a kind of scale or measure, like a thermometer or barometer, that indicates the degrees and quantities of things. The Necessary Being's absolute, all-encompassing and limitless Attributes can become known through it.

Those who know and realize that this is the reality of their essential nature and act accordingly are included in: *He is indeed prosperous who has grown it in purity (away from self-aggrandizing rebellion against God)* (91:9). Such people truly carry out the Trust and, through the telescope of self-hood, see what the universe is and what duties it performs. When any information about the universe comes to their soul, they see that their selfhood confirms it, and this information remains as light and wisdom, without changing into darkness and futility. When Selfhood has performed its duty in this way, it renounces its claim to lordship and hypothetical ownership (mere devices of measurement) and proclaims: "His is the sovereignty and ownership of all beings, and to Him is due all praise and gratitude. His is the judgment and rule, and to Him you are returning." Thus it achieves true worship and servanthood and attains the rank of the best pattern of creation.

But if Selfhood forgets the Divine purpose of its creation, abandons its duty of creation, and views itself as a self-existing being independent of the Creator, it betrays the Trust and falls into the class of those referred to in:

---

17 The *alif* is a short, vertical line representing the first letter of the Arabic alphabet and the word *ana* (I). (Tr.)

And he is indeed lost who corrupts it (91:10). This attitude or this aspect of
Selfhood is responsible for all the kinds of polytheism, evil, and deviation
that have caused the heavens, the earth, and the mountains to be terrified
of assuming the Trust—lest they might be led to associate hypothetical
partners with God.

If Selfhood, which is only an insubstantial *alif*, a thread, a hypothetical
line, is not perceived in its true essence, it grows and swells under the soil
of ignorance until it gradually permeates all parts of a human being. Like
some huge monster, it completely swallows such people so that they and
their faculties may consist of nothing more than Selfhood. Eventually, the
tribal or national zealotry and human racism give strength to the individual
selfhood. This causes it to contest, like Satan, the All-Majestic Maker's
commands. Finally taking itself as a yardstick, it compares everyone and
everything with itself, divides God's sovereignty between them and other
causes, and begins to associate partners with God in the most grievous manner. Such people are referred to in: *Surely associating partners with God is
indeed a tremendous wrong* (31:13). Just as a man who has stolen money
from the public treasury attempts to justify his action by saying that he took
a certain sum for each of his friends, so too, one who claims self-ownership
ends up believing and claiming that everything owns itself.

While in this treacherous position, Selfhood is in absolute ignorance.
Even if it has absorbed thousands of branches of science, its ignorance is
only compounded by its knowledge. For whatever glimmers of knowledge
of God its senses and reflective powers may have brought to it from the
universe, they are extinguished because it can no longer find within its
soul anything with which to confirm, polish, and maintain them. Whatever
comes to Selfhood is stained with the colors within it. Even if pure wisdom comes, it becomes absolutely futile within a selfhood stained with by
atheism, polytheism, or other forms of denying the All-Mighty. If the whole
universe were full of shining signs of God, a dark point in that selfhood
would hide them from view, as though they were invisible.

In truth, however, the essential quality proper to human nature and
to Selfhood within that nature is to point out what is other than itself. As
discussed in the Eleventh Word, true to that nature, Selfhood is a most
sensitive scale and accurate measure, a comprehensive index and perfect
map, a comprehensive mirror, and a fitting calendar and diary for the universe.

We now shed some light on the truth of this subject. Consider the following: From Adam's time until the present, two great currents or lines of thought have spread their branches in all directions and in every class of humanity, just like two tall trees. One is the line of Prophethood and religion; the other is that of philosophy and human wisdom. Whenever they agree and unite, whenever philosophy joins religion in obedience and service to it, humanity has experienced brilliant happiness and collective life. But whenever they have followed separate paths, truth and goodness have accumulated on the side of Prophethood and religion, whereas error, evil, and deviation have been drawn to the side of philosophy. We will elaborate on the origin and foundations of those two lines.

Philosophy, whenever it has split from religion, has taken the form of a tree of *Zaqqum* spreading its dark veils of ascribing partners to God and of misguidance. On the branch of the faculty of intellect or reason, it has yielded the fruits of atheism, materialism, and naturalism for the intellect's consumption. On the branch of the faculty of anger and passion, it has produced such tyrants as Nimrod, Pharaoh, and Shaddad[18] to tyrannize people. On the branch of the faculty of lusts and appetites, it has produced the fruits of goddesses, idols and those who have claimed divine status for themselves.[19]

In contrast, the blessed line of Prophethood, which takes the form of the *Touba* tree of worship, has borne the fruits of Prophets, Messengers, saints, and the righteous in the garden of the earth and on the branch of intellect. On the branch of anger and passion, the branch of defense against and repelling of evil, it has yielded the fruits of virtuous and just rulers. On the branch of attractiveness, it has borne the fruits of generous, benevolent persons of good character and modest bearing throughout history. As a result, this line has demonstrated how humanity is the perfect fruit of creation.

We will now shed light on selfhood's two aspects or faces as the origin and principal seed of these two lines of thought. One face is represented by Prophets and the other by philosophers.

---

[18] Shaddad was a tyrannical king of Antiquity who ruled in Yemen. (Tr.)

[19] The philosophies of ancient Egypt and Babylon, which either practiced magic or were thought to do so because they were represented by a small elite, produced and nurtured Nimrods and Pharaohs. The mire of naturalist philosophy gave birth to idolatry and planted deities in the ancient Greek mind. When humanity draws the veil of nature between Divine light and itself, people attribute divinity to everything and cause themselves nothing but trouble.

The face represented by Prophethood is the origin of pure worship and servitude to God, for our selfhood knows that it is His servant. Selfhood realizes that it serves One other than itself and that its essential nature has only an indicative function. It understands that it bears the meaning of one other than itself and that it can be meaningful only when it points to that One upon Whom its existence depends. Selfhood believes that its existence and life depend upon that One's Creativity and Existence. Its feeling of ownership is illusory, for selfhood knows that it enjoys only an apparent, temporary ownership by the real Owner's permission and that it has only a shadow-like reality. It is a contingent entity, an insignificant shadow manifesting the true and necessary Reality. Its duty is consciously serving as a measure and balance for its Creator's Attributes and essential Characteristics.

This is how Prophets, pure and righteous ones, and saints who follow the Prophets' line perceive selfhood's nature. As a result, they resign sovereignty to the All-Majestic Sovereign and Master of creation and believe that He has no partner or like in His Sovereignty, Lordship, and Divinity. He does not need an assistant or a deputy. In addition, He possesses the key to and has absolute power over all things. "Natural" causes are but a veil of appearances, and that nature is the sum of His creation's rules, an assemblage of His laws, of how He displays His Power.

This radiant, luminous, beautiful face of Selfhood always has been like a living seed full of meaning. From it, the All-Majestic Creator has created the *Touba* tree of worship, the blessed branches of which have adorned all parts of our world with its illustrious fruits. Through this face, the darkness over the past is removed and we understand that the past is not a domain of eternal extinction or a vast graveyard, as conceived by philosophy, but rather a source of light and a bright, shining ladder with many rungs from which all souls traversing it may leap into the future and eternal happiness. It is also a radiant abode and a garden for souls that have left this world, cast off their heavy loads, and been set free.

The second face, represented by philosophy, regards Selfhood as having an essential meaning of its own. It says that Selfhood has an independent existence, is an index only to itself, and labors wholly on its own behalf. It considers Selfhood's existence as necessary and essential, and falsely assumes that selfhood owns its being and is the real lord and master of its own domain. Philosophy supposes Selfhood to be a permanent reality that has, as its duty, the quest for self-perfection for the sake of self-esteem.

As a result of such mistaken views, philosophers have built their schools of thought on corrupt foundations. Even such eminent philosophers as Plato and Aristotle, Ibn Sina (Avicenna) and al-Farabi (Alfarabius), maintained that people's ultimate aim is to make themselves like the Necessary Being; in other words, to actually resemble Him. Such views provoked Selfhood and set it free to run in the valleys of polytheism. This opened the way to associating partners with God via such practices as the worship of causes, idols, natural forces, and stars. They closed the doors to people's perception and confession of their innate impotence and weakness, insufficiency and need, deficiency and imperfection, and thus blocked the road to worship and servitude to God. Immersed in naturalism and unable to escape from ascribing partners to God, they could not locate the wide open doors of gratitude.

In contrast, Prophethood considered that humanity's aim and duty is to be molded by Divine values and achieve good character. Prophets believed that people should perceive their impotence and seek refuge with Divine Power, perceive their weakness and rely on Divine Strength, realize their insufficiency and essential poverty and trust in Divine Mercy, know their need and seek help from Divine Riches, see their faults and plead for pardon through Divine Forgiveness, and perceive their inadequacy and glorify Divine Perfection.

Philosophy's deviation from the Straight Path, in disobedience to religion, caused Selfhood to take up the reins and gallop into error. Consequently, a tree of *Zaqqum* has grown out of such selfhood and swallowed up more than half of humanity. The fruits it has presented on the branch of lusts and appetites are idols and female deities, for according to the principles of philosophy, power is approved. "Might is right" is the norm. Its maxims are: "All power to the strongest"; "Winner takes all," and "In power there is right."[20] It has given moral support to tyranny, encouraged dictators, and urged oppressors to claim divinity. By ascribing the beauty in "works of Art" and the threads of which they are made to the works and threads themselves, and not to the Maker and Fashioner's pure, sacred Beauty, it says: "How beautiful it is," not: "How beautifully made it is," and thus considers each as an idol worthy of adoration.

In addition, philosophy adulates a cheap, self-conceited, ostentatious, superficial, transient, physical beauty that may be sold to anyone. This has

---

[20] The principle of Prophethood says: "Power is inherent in right; right is not inherent in power." It thus halts tyranny and secures justice.

led people into pretension and caused these new "idols" to display hypocritical reverence before their admirers.[21] On the branch of anger and passion, it has nurtured the fruits of greater and lesser Nimrods, Pharaohs, and Shaddads to tyrannize unfortunate people. On the branch of intellect or reason, it has yielded such fruits as atheism, materialism, and naturalism, all of which it has embedded into the human mind and thereby thrown people into confusion. To clarify this truth, we will give a few examples and compare the results originating from Prophethood's sound foundations with those arising from philosophy's rotten foundations.

FIRST EXAMPLE: According to one of Prophethood's principles concerning individual life, namely, the rule: "Be molded by Divine values," there is the instruction: "Seek distinction through Divine values and turn toward the All-Mighty with humility, recognizing your impotence and insufficiency, and be a servant in His Court." But philosophy, due to its self-oriented principle of seeking human perfection in being like the Necessarily Existent Being, instructs: "Try to be like the Necessarily Existent Being." This is impossible, for while the Necessarily Existent Being is infinitely powerful, omnipotent, self-sufficient, and without need, our essence has been mixed with infinite impotence, weakness, poverty, and need.

SECOND EXAMPLE: Among Prophethood's principles of social life's fundamental conditions are mutual assistance, magnanimity, and generosity. These function in the reciprocal cooperation of all things—from the sun and the moon down to particles. For example, plants help animals, animals help people, and particles of food help the body's cells. Philosophy, however, considers conflict to be social life's fundamental condition. In fact, conflict springs from tyrants, brutes, and savage people and wild animals misusing their innate dispositions. Conflict is so fundamental and general to the philosophers' line of reasoning that they absurdly claim that "life is conflict."

THIRD EXAMPLE: One sublime result and exalted principle of Prophethood about Divine Unity is: "That which has unity can proceed only from one (of unity)." That is, the unity and universal accord or harmony in existence is because of the Creator's Oneness. Whereas philosophy states that "Only one proceeds from one." Thus, as only one thing can proceed from one per-

---

21 In order to appear desirable to their admirers and gain their attention, such people display a kind of "worshipful" attitude through a hypocritical show.

son, everything comes from that one by means of intermediaries. This misleading principle opened the way to a most grievous polytheism. By presenting the absolutely All-Powerful and Self-Sufficient as needing impotent intermediaries, it gave all causes and intermediaries a kind of partnership in His Lordship and allotted only the creation of the "First Intellect" to the All-Majestic Creator. If the Illuminists (*Ishraqiyyun*), considered among the foremost of philosophers, exerted themselves for such nonsense, just imagine how absurd are the theories of such inferior philosophers as materialists and naturalists.

FOURTH EXAMPLE: According to one of Prophethood's wise principles that *There is nothing but it glorifies Him with His praise* (17:44), the purpose and wisdom in creation, particularly of living creatures, may have one aspect relating to the creature itself but many aspects relating to the Creator. For example, a fruit has as much wisdom and as many purposes involved in its creation as all fruits of a tree. However, according to philosophy's principles, which lack true wisdom, every living creature's purpose relates to itself or is connected with benefits for humanity. This means that creation is so senseless that the purpose of a mountain-like tree is only to yield a tiny fruit. It is one of the disastrous results of philosophy that such great Muslim philosophers as Ibn Sina and al-Farabi, infatuated by philosophy's apparent glamour and deceived into following it, were considered only ordinary believers. *Hujjatu'l-Islam* al-Ghazzali did not accord them even that rank.

The leaders of the Mu'tazili school, who were among the most learned scholars of Islamic theology, were attracted by philosophy's glitter and became closely involved with it. Considering reason to be a self-sufficient and sound measure for determining the truth, they could not rise above the rank of heretical or novitiate belief. Furthermore, since they took pleasure in philosophy's flattery of their evil-commanding souls, such famous literary figures in Islamic history as Abu'l-A'la al-Ma'arri, notorious for his pessimism, and Omar Khayyam, known for his pitiful weeping, basked in philosophy's applause. However, they earned contempt, condemnation, and restraining reproofs from people of truth and perfection, who told them: "You are being impertinent. You are approaching heresy and leading others to heresy."

Another consequence of philosophy's rotten basis is that Selfhood, instead of being viewed as insubstantial, is seen as self-regarding and self-dependent. This view has caused it to change from a "light vapor" into a "viscous liquid." Due to our indifference to creation's miraculous truths (as we now are "too familiar" with them) and our preoccupation with this world and natural sciences, that liquid hardens. After this, due to our neglect and denial, Selfhood "freezes." It loses its refinement and becomes opaque, due to its rebelliousness, gradually becoming denser and enveloping the person. It then expands with all sorts of human fancies.

Finally supposing all people and even causes to be like itself—though they deny it—it considers each one a Pharaoh. At this point, it contests the All-Majestic Creator's commands: *Who will revive these bones when they have rotted away?* (36:78) and, in defiance, accuses the absolutely All-Powerful of impotence. Selfhood even goes so far as to debase the All-Majestic Creator's Attributes by rejecting or deforming the Attributes it deems unsuited to its interest or disagreeable to its Pharaoh-like evil-commanding soul.

For example, some philosophers considered the All-Mighty "self-bound" (i.e., constrained by His own decree) and thus denied Him choice. They rejected creation's endless testimony which proves that He has choice. Although all creatures show that the Creator has choice, each with its own individuality and order, wisdom and measure, this blind philosophy refuses to see it. Other philosophers claimed that Divine Knowledge does not contain the particulars, thereby denying the Attribute of all-encompassing Knowledge and refusing to accept creation's true witnessing.

Philosophy also has attributed a creative effect to causes and thereby attributing creative power to nature. Since it does not see the clear stamp upon everything signifying the Creator of all things, philosophy assumes nature to be the originator. It ignores the facts that nature, whose supposed power is ascribed to blind chance and necessity, is impotent, inanimate, unconscious, and blind. It attributes a part of creation to nature, although every element is but a missive from God, the Eternally Besought, relaying thousands of instances of exalted wisdom.

Moreover, philosophers did not find the door to the Resurrection and the Hereafter, which the All-Mighty (with all of His Names), the universe (with all of its truths), the line of Prophethood (with all of its verifications), and the revealed Books (with all of their verses) demonstrate. As a result, they denied bodily resurrection and ascribed pre-eternity to souls. Such superstitions give an idea of what their views on other matters would be. Indeed, the powers of evil have raised up (flattered) the intellects or reason of disbelieving philosophers as though with the beaks and talons of their ego or selfhood and thrown them into the abyss of deviation. In the microcosm (human), they have made Ego or Selfhood into an idol or a false deity; in the macrocosm, they have made nature an object of worship. *Hence, he who rejects the false deities (and powers of evil which institute patterns of faith and rule in defiance of God) and believes in God has indeed taken hold of the firm, unbreakable handle; and God is All-Hearing, All-Knowing* (2:256).

It is useful to mention here, to elucidate the aforementioned truth, the meaning of an imaginary event I described as a visionary journey in Gleams of Truth. In İstanbul, eight years before I wrote this treatise, during Ramadan, at a time when the Old Said (concerned with philosophy) was about to become the New Said, while pondering over the three ways indicated at the end of *Suratu'l-Fatiha—The Path of those whom You have favored, not of those who have incurred (Your) wrath, nor of those who are astray* (1: 7)—I saw the following:

I was in a vast desert. The earth's face was covered by a layer of murky, depressing, and suffocating clouds. There was no breeze, light, or water. I imagined that dangerous and dreadful monsters were everywhere. It occurred to me that there should be a light, a breeze, and some water at the other side of this land, and I should get there. I noticed that I was driven on involuntarily. Worming my way into an underground tunnel-like cave and gradually traveling through the earth, I saw that many people had passed this way before me. They were submerged on all sides. Sometimes I saw their footprints and heard their voices, which later ceased.

> O friend who is with me on this imaginary journey. That land is nature and the philosophy of nature-worship. The tunnel is the way opened by philosophical thought to reach the truth. The footprints belonged to famous philosophers like Plato and Aristotle, and the voices I heard were those of such geniuses as Ibn Sina and al-Farabi.[22] I occasionally encountered some of Ibn Sina's ideas and principles but, after a time, they would disappear completely. Being

---

[22] If asked: "Who are you to challenge these famous philosophers? While you are like a fly, how dare you challenge the flight of eagles?" I would reply: "I have an eternal teacher like the Qur'an, and so, in matters of the truth and knowledge of God, do not need to attach as much value as a gnat's wing to such eagles, who were students of misguided philosophy and deluded reason. However inferior I am to them, their teacher is far more inferior than mine. With the help of my "teacher"—the Qur'an—nature and materialistic tendencies that led them to drown cannot even wet my toes. An insignificant private who serves a great ruler's laws and commands can achieve more than an insignificant ruler's chief general."

unable to proceed, he was submerged before reaching the truth. Anyhow, I showed you a small part of the truth to save you from anxiety. Now I return to my journey.

As I went on, I found that I had been given two things: a torch to dispel the darkness and a device that was opening a way for me through mighty boulders and rocks, which fell apart one after the other. I was told: "This torch and device have been given to you from the treasury of the Qur'an." After continuing on for a long time, I suddenly realized that I had come out on the other side. I saw a world where everything was rejoicing, and which had bright sunshine in the most beautiful springtime and an enlivening breeze and delicious life-giving water. I thanked and praised God.

Then I realized that instead of being in command of myself, I was being tested by someone. I again found myself under the suffocating cloud in that vast desert. Though now on another path, I still felt urged on by an unseen motive. This time I was traveling on the earth's surface to reach the other side. I saw things so strange and curious that they cannot be described: raging seas, threatening storms—everything caused difficulties for me. As before, I felt my way through them with the help of the equipment that had been given to me from the Qur'an, and so overcame all of them. On the way, I frequently encountered the corpses of other travelers. Barely one in a thousand had completed this journey. However, I was saved from that suffocating cloud and came out the other side, happily, in full view of the shining sun. I breathed in the enlivening breeze and said: "All praise be to God."

Then I started looking around that Paradise-like world. But someone would not let me stay there, for instantly I was returned to that dreadful desert as if I had to see another path. There I saw different sorts of apparatuses—some like airplanes, others like cars and hoists—all of which had descended like lifts. Those who jumped onto them were taken up as far as their power and capacity allowed. I jumped onto one of them, and, in a moment, was raised high above the cloud. I came out among the most beautiful, green, and spectacular mountain tops. The cloud layer only reached halfway up the mountains, and mild breezes, delicious water, and gentle light were everywhere, as were those lift-like luminous vehicles. Although I had seen them in the first two parts of my journey and on the earth's other face, I had not understood what they were. Now I came to realize that they were manifestations of the All-Wise Qur'an's verses.

The first way, indicated by *nor of those who are astray*, is that of people sunk in the bog of nature and followers of naturalism. You have seen how many difficulties this way contains. The second way, indicated by *not of those who have incurred Your wrath*, is followed by those who attribute creative power and creative effect to causes and intermediaries, and those (like the Peripatetic philosophers) who seek to open the way to the ultimate truth and knowledge of the Necessarily Existent Being through reasoning and thinking alone. The third way, indicated by *those whom You have favored*, it is the radiant highway of those who follow the Qur'an, the people of the Straight Path. This radiant highway is a brilliant path revealed and bestowed by God, the All-Merciful. It is the shortest, easiest, and safest way, and is open to everyone.

The Twenty-second Word

The way of destruction and the way of happiness

In the Name of God, the All-Merciful, the All-Compassionate.

EFT WITHOUT ANY SUPPORT, THE REPRESENTATIVE OF THE MISGUIDED reveals his or her real intention: "Since I find worldly pleasure, happiness, and advancement in civilization in denying God and the Hereafter, in loving this world, and in human freedom and self-confidence, I bring others to this path, with Satan's help, and will continue to do so."

ANSWER: I say in the Qur'an's name: O helpless fellow, come to your senses and do not listen to the representative of the misguided. If you do, you will suffer such loss that the spirit, mind and heart shudder even to imagine it. There are two paths before you: the path of wretchedness offered by the representative of the misguided and the path of happiness described in the Qur'an. You have already seen many comparisons between these two paths in *The Words*, primarily in the first nine short ones. Now heed only one among a thousand, which befits the occasion:

The path of associating partners with God and other kinds of misguidance, and of transgression and dissipation causes us to fall to bottomless depths of degradation. It places an unbearable load on our weak backs and burdens our hearts with boundless sorrow. For if we do not recognize and place our trust in Almighty God, we become like very weak, impotent, infinitely poor, and destitute animals, or mortal beings afflicted with pain and grief, subject to countless calamities. We suffer incessantly, for we remain separated from all things and people that we have loved and to which we have been connected. Leaving all things and people amidst the pain of separation, we enter the grave's dark depths alone.

We struggle in vain, with a limited will, little power, a short life-span, and a dull mind against infinite pain and ambition. We strive to realize our countless desires and goals, but without any considerable result. While we cannot bear even the burden of our own being, we load our minds and backs with the burden of the world. We suffer Hell's torments even before going to it.

In order to avoid feeling such a painful spiritual torment, people of misguidance seek out heedlessness as a kind of anesthesia. But they begin to feel this pain most acutely as they approach the grave. Not being true servants of Almighty God, they believe that they own themselves. In reality, however, with their limited free will and insignificant power, they cannot govern their being in this tumultuous world. They encounter many enemies from harmful microbes to earthquakes ready to attack them. They look at the grave in fear and terror.

As human beings, they are related to humanity and the world. But since they deny that the world and humanity belong to and under the authority of the One Who is the All-Wise, the All-Knowing, the All-Powerful, the All-Compassionate, and the All-Munificent, they attribute their existence and lives to chance and nature. And so the world's fearful events (e.g., convulsions, earthquakes, plagues, calamity, death, and famine) and humanity's conditions and experiences always trouble them. Moreover, they must contend with their own pain and the troubles that other creatures cause them to suffer.

As their own unbelief brought them to this deplorable state, how can they deserve mercy and affection? This reminds us of The Eighth Word's parable of two brothers who fell into two wells. If one, without being content with a fine banquet's agreeable and lawful enjoyment and entertainment among honest friends in a beautiful garden, drinks wine to obtain an unlawful pleasure and, imagining themselves surrounded by wild beasts in a dirty place on a winter day, trembles and cries in fear, they will not deserve pity. For they see their honest friends as wild beasts and insult them. They see delicious food as foul; clean, fine plates and bowls as worthless, dirty stones; and attempt to break them. Moreover, they judge the invaluable, meaningful books that they are to read and study as ordinary, meaningless collections of sheets, and tear them up and scatter them. Such people are not merely unworthy of pity, rather, they deserve to be punished.

Similarly, unbelief and misguidance arise from abusing one's willpower. Such people assert that the All-Wise Maker's guest-house of the world is a plaything of chance and nature and that the transference of beings to the

World of the Unseen, after completing their duty of refreshing the Divine Names' manifestations, is going into absolute non-existence. Also, they judge beings' glorifications and recitations of the Divine Names as outcries of death and eternal separation; sheets of creatures, each being a missive of the Eternally Besought, to be confused, meaningless collections; the grave's door, which opens onto the World of Mercy, as opening onto a dark world of non-existence; and death as separation from—not re-union with—all friends and beloved ones. Thus, they deliver themselves to an extremely painful punishment. Since they also deny, reject, and insult all creatures, the Divine Names, and His inscriptions and missives, they deserve punishment. They are in no way worthy of pity.

So, unfortunate people of misguidance and dissipation, can any of your progress, evolution, science, technology, and civilization compensate for such a terrible loss, collapse, and crushing hopelessness? Where can you find the true consolation that the human spirit urgently needs above all else? What nature or causality, what thing upon which you rely and to which you attribute His works, bounties, and favors, which of your discoveries, inventions, idols, and fetishes can save you from the darkness of death, which you suppose to be eternal extinction? Which one can take you through the Intermediate World of the grave, the Place of Resurrection and Supreme Gathering, and over the Bridge to the Abode of eternal happiness? Since you cannot close the grave's door, you are bound to travel and tread this way (passing through the stations mentioned.) To travel it safely, you must depend on the One Who commands and controls all those worlds and abodes.

O unfortunate, misguided, and heedless people. Any love directed to other than that which deserves it brings suffering. In view of this, misusing the potential of loving and knowing given to you to know and love God and His Attributes and Names, you love your selves and the world. This, as well as your similar misuse of your body and faculties that were given so that you could worship and thank Him, causes you to suffer deserved punishment. Assigning to your selves the love that must be felt for Almighty God, you suffer the resulting troubles. You are suffering the endless troubles that your own selves cause you. You do not provide true peace and happiness for what you adore: your soul or self. Since you do not submit and entrust it to the Absolutely Powerful One, the True Beloved One, you always suffer pain.

Since you assign the love belonging to Almighty God's Names and Attributes to the world and attribute the works of His Art to causality and nature, you are suffering the resulting pains. That which you love either leaves you without saying good-bye or does not recognize you. Even if it recognizes you, it does not love you. Even if it loves you, it gives you no benefit. You always suffer from incessant separation and death without hope of re-union.

This is the reality of what the people of misguidance call the happiness of life and human perfection, beauty of civilization, and pleasure of freedom. Dissipation and drunkenness temporarily veil the suffering and pain that eventually will come upon them.

As for the Qur'an's light-diffusing way, it heals the wounds afflicting the misguided with the truths of belief, disperses the darkness enveloping them, and closes the doors of misguidance and perdition.

This way removes our weakness, impotence, poverty, and need, for it enables us to trust in an All-Powerful One of Compassion. Submitting the burden of being and life to His Power and Mercy, we are saved from their mount; instead, we transform the self and life into a mount for us. We learn that we are true human beings and the All-Merciful One's welcomed guests, not "speaking animals." Showing the world as the All-Merciful One's guest-house, and its creatures as mirrors of Divine Names and ever-recruited missives of the Eternally Besought, it heals perfectly all our wounds caused by the transience of the world, the decay of things, and love for mortals. It also saves us from the darkness of whims and fancies. Also, showing life as the prelude to re-union with deceased friends and beloved ones, it heals the wounds of death, which the misguided regard as eternal separation, and shows that separation is actually re-union.

By proving that the grave is a door opened onto the World of Mercy, the Abode of Happiness, the gardens of Paradise, and the luminous Realm of the All-Merciful One, the way of the Qur'an removes our greatest fear and shows that our journey in the Intermediate World, which seems to be most depressing and troublesome, is really most pleasant and exhilarating. It demonstrates that the grave is not like a dragon's mouth, but rather a door opened onto the gardens of Divine Mercy. It informs believers:

> If your willpower is very limited, entrust your affairs to your Owner's universal Will. If your power is slight and insignificant, rely on the Absolutely Powerful One's Power. If your life is short, consider eter-

nal life. If your mind is dull, come into the Qur'an's sun, and look with the light of belief, so that in place of your mind, which gives light like a firefly, each Qur'anic verse gives you light like a most shining star. If you have endless ambition and pain, boundless reward and infinite mercy await you. If you have limitless desire and aims, do not be anxious, for you cannot realize all of them here. This is only possible in another realm, and the One Who gives them to you is not your self.

And:

You do not own yourself, but are owned by One infinitely Powerful and an infinitely Compassionate One of Majesty. So, do not trouble yourself by placing your being and life on your shoulders, for the One Who has given and governs your life is He. Also, the world is not without an owner. So do not be anxious thinking of the state of it and load that burden onto your mind, for the world's Owner is All-Wise and All-Knowing. You are His guest in His world, so do not interfere with what is beyond your power and responsibility. Such living beings like humanity and animals are not left to themselves. Rather, they are officials charged with certain duties and are controlled and favored by an All-Wise, All-Compassionate One. He has far more compassion for them than for you. Furthermore, from microbes to catastrophes like plagues, floods, droughts, and earthquakes, which, in appearance, are hostile to you, all things and events are controlled and governed by that All-Compassionate, All-Wise One. He is the All-Wise and so does nothing useless, and the All-Compassionate Whose every act contains a kind of grace.

It adds:

This transient world provides the necessities of the afterlife. It decays, but yields everlasting fruits and displays an All-Permanent One's Eternal Names. In return for its few pleasures, it causes one to suffer many pains and afflictions. However, the favors of the All-Merciful, All-Compassionate One are true and lasting pleasures, and its pains cause one to obtain many spiritual rewards. What is lawful is sufficient for the spirit's enjoyment and pleasures, as well as for the heart and carnal soul, so do not enter upon what is unlawful. Any illicit pleasure results in numerous pains and causes one to lose the All-Merciful One's favors, which are pure, lasting pleasures.

Misguidance so debases humanity that no philosophic trend, scientific development, or human civilization and progress can lift people out of that deep pit of darkness. It is only the wise Qur'an that it takes us out of the lowest pit and raises us to the highest rank through belief and righteous deeds. It fills that deep pit with the steps of spiritual progress and the means of spiritual perfection.

The Qur'an also facilitates our long, troubling, and stormy journey toward eternity. It shows us how to traverse in a day the distance that normally takes fifty thousand years to cover. By enabling us to know the the All-Majestic Being, the King of all eternity, it honors us with being His dutiful servants and guests and secures for us an easy and comfortable journey through the world and through the mansions of the Intermediate World of the grave and the Hereafter.

Just as a king's righteous, dutiful official travels in his domain in security, via the fastest modes of transportation, and easily cross provincial boundaries, so those connected with the Eternal King through belief, as well as those who show obedience to Him through righteous deeds, travel through the stations and across the boundaries of the world and the realms of the grave and the Hereafter with the speed of lightning or Buraq, the mount of Paradise. Such people find eternal happiness. The Qur'an proves the truth of this, and purified religious scholars and saints see it clearly.

The Qur'an also says:

> O believers, do not waste your God-given infinite capacity of loving on your ugly, defective, evil, and harmful carnal soul. Do not adore it or follow its desires and fancies as if it were an object of worship, but direct it toward the One worthy of infinite love, Who does you infinite good and will make you infinitely happy; Who through His favors makes happy those with whom you have connections and whose happiness pleases you; One with infinite perfection and infinitely sacred, transcendent, pure, perfect, and undecaying beauty; Whose every Name radiates numerous lights of beauty and grace; the beauty of Whose Mercy and the mercy of Whose Beauty are displayed in Paradise; and Whose Beauty and Perfection all the beauty, grace, and perfection in the universe, which are lovable, point to and signal. Love Him, and make Him the sole object of your worship.

Furthermore it says:

> O humanity, do not use your infinite capacity of loving, which has been given to you to love His Names and Attributes, to love impermanent beings. All that exists, except for Him, is transitory, whereas the Divine All-Beautiful Names displayed on mortals are permanent and constant. Each Name and Attribute has thousands of degrees of

favoring and thousands of levels of perfection and love. Consider, for example, the Name the All-Merciful: Paradise is one of Its manifestations, eternal happiness is one of Its radiances, and all provisions and bounties bestowed on worldly creatures are just one of Its drops.

To see how the Qur'an expresses the difference between these two ways, consider: *Surely We have created humanity of the best stature as the perfect pattern of creation; then We reduced it to the lowest of the low, save those who believe and do good, rihgteous deeds* (95:4–6); and *Neither the heavens nor the earth wept over their destruction* (44:29). See in what elevated and miraculous style they express the difference! A detailed explanation of the first verse can be found in The Eleventh Word. Here we present a few remarks on the exalted truth contained in the other verse, which explicitly states that the heavens and the earth do not weep when unbelievers die. This implies that the heavens and the earth weep when believers die.

Unbelievers do not know the meaning of the heavens and the earth, do not recognize their Maker, deny their duties, and so reduce their value. Such insults and hostility cause the heavens and the earth to be pleased when such people die. But they weep when believers die, for believers know the duties of the heavens and the earth and affirm the reality they bear. As their belief enlightens them about these meanings, they say: "How beautifully they have been created. How well they perform their duties." Believers acknowledge their value and respect them accordingly. They also love them and the Names to which they are mirrors in Almighty God's name. And so the heavens and the earth grieve for them.

The First Gleam

Taking refuge in God with the supplication of the Prophet Jonah

In the Name of God, the All-Merciful, the All-Compassionate.

ECITING THE QUR'ANIC VERSES AND THE PHRASES BELOW EACH thirty-three times, particularly between the Evening Prayer and the Nightfall Prayer is of great merit. The first is about the Prophet Jonah, upon him be peace.

Eventually he called out in the veils of darkness (formed of the belly of the fish, the sea, and dark, rainy night): "There is no deity but You, All-Glorified are You (in that You are absolutely above having any defect). Surely I have been one of the wrongdoers (who have wronged themselves)." (21:87)

He called out to his Lord, saying, "Truly, affliction has visited me (so that I can no longer worship You as I must); and You are the Most Merciful of the merciful." (21:83)

Still, if they turn away from you (O Messenger), say: "God is sufficient for me; there is no deity but He. In Him have I put my trust, and He is the Lord of the Supreme Throne (as the absolute Ruler and Sustainer of the universe and all creation, Who maintains and protects it)." (9:129)

God is sufficient for us; how excellent a Guardian is He! (3:173)

There is no power and strength save with God, the All-High, the All-Mighty.

O the Everlasting, You are the Everlasting, O the Everlasting, You are the Everlasting!

For those who believe, it is guidance and healing. (41:44)

The supplication of the Prophet Jonah, upon him and our Prophet be peace and blessings, is a most powerful supplication, and a most effective means to receive an answer to our prayers from God. What follows is a summary of the well-known experience of the Prophet Jonah, upon him be peace.

He was cast into the sea, and a large fish swallowed him. The sea was stormy, and the night turbulent and dark; there was no sign of hope from any direction. While in that situation, he prayed:

> There is no deity but You, All-Glorified are You. Surely I have been one of the wrongdoers.

This supplication was a swift means of salvation for him. The power of his prayer lies in what follows:

In that situation there was no apparent means or causes to which Jonah could have had recourse for salvation; he was in need of one who could command the whale and the sea, and the night and the sky if he were to be saved. The night, the sea, and the whale were united against him. Only one who could subject all three of these to their command could bring Jonah forth on the shore of salvation. Even if all of creation had become Jonah's servants and helpers, this would have been of no avail.

This means that apparent means and causes have no part of their own in the production of results. Since Jonah saw with the eye of certainty that there was no refuge other than the Causer of Causes, and as he, through his utmost conviction of God's absolute Oneness and His dominion over the universe, fully perceived that in addition to His overall manifestations that reign supreme over all of creation, God also has manifestations particular to each thing and being as the All-Compassionate, his supplication served to be a means for the night, the sea, and the whale to be subjected to him. Through the light of his conviction of the Oneness of God, Who has absolute control over everything, the belly of the whale became a submarine for him, and the awesome sea roaring with mountain-like waves became a peaceful plain, a pleasant place for an excursion. His supplication, based on and proclaiming God's Oneness, also served for the sky to be cleared of all clouds and for the moon to shine over his head like a lantern. Those things that had been pressing him from all sides, threatening him, now showed to him a friendly face. So he reached the shore of salvation, where under a gourd plant he fully perceived the great extent to which his Lord had favored him.

Now we are in a situation one hundred times more awful than that in which the Prophet Jonah, upon him be peace, first found himself. Our night is the future. When we look upon our future with heedlessness towards our religious responsibilities, it is a hundred times darker and more fearful than his night. Our sea is this moving, unstable earth. Each wave of this sea bears on it thousands of dead bodies, and so is a thousand times more frightening than his sea. Our fish consists of the lusts and caprices of our evil-commanding soul, which strive to destroy our eternal life. Such a fish is a thousand times more harmful than his. For his fish could have destroyed a hundred-year lifespan, whereas ours seeks to destroy a life that will last hundreds of millions of years.

This being our true state, we should do as the Prophet Jonah, upon him be peace, did; turning away from all means and causes, we should take refuge directly in our Lord, Who is the Causer of Causes. We should say:

> There is no deity but You, All-Glorified are You. Surely I have been one of the wrongdoers.

We should understand and know with a certainty which comes from observation that only He, our Lord, Who keeps the future under His command, the world under His absolute control, and our evil-commanding souls under His direction, can remove from us the harm of the future, this world, and the lusts and caprices of our evil-commanding souls, all of which are united against us because of our neglect and misguidance.

What agent is there other than the Creator of the heavens and earth who can know whatever occurs in our heart, down to its most subtle and secret thoughts, and illuminate the future for us by establishing the Hereafter, saving us from the countless suffocating waves of the world? Nothing, no one other than the Necessarily Existent One can in any way help us or save us; we can only be saved with His will and permission.

As this was the case, the result of Jonah's prayers was that the whale became a mount or a vessel for him and the sea became a peaceful plain; the night was serenely lit for him by the moon. We too should then make the same supplication:

> There is no deity but You, All-Glorified are You. Surely I have been one of the wrongdoers.

With the sentence *There is no deity but You*, we should ask for God's mercy upon our future; with the phrase *All-Glorified are You* we should ask for mercy upon our world; with the phrase *Surely I have been one of the wrongdoers (who have wronged themselves)*, we should ask for mercy upon our souls. Thus, our future may be illuminated with the light of belief in an atmosphere that is lit by the Qur'an, and the awe and dread of our night may be transformed into serenity and joy. Also, while we travel this earth amidst the waves of years and centuries, a sea on which countless beings have embarked, and one out of which countless ones have been thrown into nothingness through the alternation of life and death, we should board the vessel of the truth of Islam, constructed in the dockyards of the wise Qur'an, so that we may fulfill our duty of life on the shore of safety and salvation. The tempest and turbulence of the sea will become a series of pleasing, ever-renewed spectacles, like the changing scenes on a screen, and instead of instilling fearful loneliness and dread they will enlighten our minds and urge us to take a reflective look on everything around us and to learn from the lessons. By virtue of the guidance of the Qur'an and the education that the Criterion of Truth and Falsehood gives, our soul will no longer ride us, but will instead become our mount. As we ride it, it will serve us to attain eternal life.

In short, humans have a comprehensive nature; as we suffer from and shiver with the infection of malaria, so also do we suffer from the quakes and tremors of the earth, and will also suffer from the mighty convulsions that all of creation will undergo on the Day of Resurrection. As we fear a microscopic organism, we also fear a shooting star that appears among the heavenly bodies. As we love our home, we also love the entire world. As we love our little garden, we also love the infinite and eternal Paradise, and we love this ardently. Therefore, such a being's object of worship, the Lord, our refuge, our savior, and our goal can only be the One in Whose grasp of Power is the whole universe, and under Whose command are both the atoms and planets, at one and the same time. Human beings therefore need to constantly pray, saying like Jonah, upon him be peace:

> There is no deity but You, All-Glorified are You. Surely I have been one of the wrongdoers.

> All-Glorified are You. We have no knowledge save what You have taught us. Surely You are the All-Knowing, the All-Wise.

The Seventeenth Gleam

The second Europe and the Qur'an's students

In the Name of God, the All-Merciful, the All-Compassionate.

INCE WESTERN SCIENCE AND CIVILIZATION HAD SOME DEGREE OF influence on Old Said's thought, when New Said began journeying in the mind and heart, they caused disease of the heart and great difficulties. For this reason, when New Said wanted to shake off that erroneous philosophy and degenerate civilization from his mind, in order to silence the suggestions and whisperings of his evil-commanding soul, which testified in favor of Europe, he felt compelled to hold the following discussion, which in one respect is very brief and in another is long, with the collective personality of Europe.

It should not be misunderstood; Europe is two. One is that which, benefiting from the religion of Jesus and Islamic civilization, serves human social life and justice through its scientific and technological inventions, the other is that which is based on naturalistic and materialistic philosophy and, supposing the evils of civilization to be virtues, has driven humankind to vice and misguidance. While journeying in spirit at that time, I said to this second collective personality of Europe, which holds in its hand useless, harmful philosophy and dissolute civilization in the place of beneficial sciences and the virtues of civilization:

Know, O second Europe! You have taken in your right hand dark, deviating philosophy and in your left hand corrupt, harmful civilization. Then you claim that humanity's happiness lies in them. I wish your hands would be broken and that your two offerings would cause you to die.

O you wretched spirit, which spreads unbelief and ingratitude! Can one with a corrupt conscience and suffering from mental or spiritual illnesses be happy with rich clothes, superficial, deceptive glitter, and worldly possessions? Do you not see that for one who is disappointed or disillu-sioned by the non-fulfillment of every expectation, sweetness turns sour, pleasure changes into pain, and the world becomes narrow? How can one exposed to your evil, whose heart and spirit have been stricken with your misguidance and left frustrated and distressed, find happiness with what you offer? Can one be described as happy when their body is in a deceiv-ing, fleeting paradisiacal state or while their spirit and heart are in hellish torment? See, you have led astray wretched humanity in this way, and caused them hellish sufferings in a false paradise.

O evil-commanding soul of humankind! Consider the following para-ble and see where you have driven humankind. There are two roads before us. We choose one and begin to walk. At every step helpless people are attacked by thugs who rob them of everything, destroy their houses, and beat them so savagely that even heaven weeps for them. Wherever we look we see the same scene, filled with the shouts of the oppressors and the cries and lamentations of the oppressed. Since we feel pain when others are in pain, our conscience cannot bear such injustice or laments. So, those who see such events will either abandon all human feelings and, no longer concerned with the destruction of others as long as they themselves remain safe, surrender to the utmost degree of savagery, or utterly ignore the demands of the heart and reason.

O Europe, corrupted with vice and misguidance and taken far from the religion of Jesus! You have used your genius which, like the *Dajjal*,[23] has only a single eye, to bring humanity to this hellish state as a "gift" and then, seeing that this illness is so incurable that it casts humankind from the high-est of the high to the lowest of the low, reducing them to the basest level of bestiality, you offer people charming amusements and fancies as a cure to anaesthetize them. However, your cure will kill you. The road you have opened up for humankind and the happiness you have given them resemble the first road in the parable.

The other road, which the wise Qur'an has bestowed on humankind, is this: We see that at every station, place, and town, the soldiers of a just sov-ereign perform their duties. Now and then the sovereign's officials come,

---

[23] The *Dajjal* (the Anti-Christ in the Christian tradition) is the person or persons or a move-ment that claims the non-existence of God, extremely opposes religion and tries to eradi-cate it from people's life. (Tr.)

take the weapons and other belongings lent to them by the government, and give them their discharge papers. The soldiers are pleased, although outwardly they look sad because the horses and weapons which they love have been taken back; but now they can visit the sovereign and return to the capital of his country. If the demobilization officials meet a recruit who does not know them and they ask him to surrender his weapons, that recruit tells them, "I am the sovereign's soldier and in his service. My final destination is with him. If he has sent you here, welcome. If not, stay away, for no matter how many of you there are, I will fight with you—not for myself, because I do not own myself, I belong to my sovereign: both my self and my weapons are in trust from my owner. So I shall not submit to you but shall preserve my sovereign's trust and protect his royal dignity and honor."

This is only one of the thousands of instances of joy and happiness on the second road. Throughout the journey, we constantly see new troops gathered or mobilized with joy and celebrations under the name of birth, while many others are discharged with cheers and military bands under the name of death. The wise Qur'an has offered humanity this road as a gift. If people respect it and use it as a guide, they will enter this second road. *Then no fear shall come upon them, neither shall they grieve* (10:62).

O second, corrupted Europe! A number of your rotten and baseless foundations are as follows. You say, "All living creatures, from the greatest angel to the tiniest fish, are their own lords; they work in their own name, and strive for their own pleasure. They have the right to life, and their only aim in life is to survive." Do you not see the universal mutual helping among them, established by their All-Munificent Creator as a principle of munificence which is perfectly obeyed in all the spheres of the universe? Plants help animals, and animals help humanity. But, supposing that the compassionate, munificent manifestations of this universal law of mutual assistance are conflict and contention, you preach that life consists of conflict. How can this be true? Can you not see that the particles or atoms of all food help to nourish the body's cells? This mutual assistance results from everything obeying the order of a Munificent Lord, and proves that no living creature is the lord of itself. But another rotten foundation of yours is that you say, "Everything owns itself or is its own lord." Another clear proof that nothing owns itself is this: Among all living agents, the most honorable, and the one endowed with the most extensive will and the widest field of activity is humanity. Despite this, our part even in our daily acts, like thinking, speaking, and eating, which we do by our will and power, is minuscule. So how can those who do not own even one hundredth of their most ordinary acts such as these, claim ownership and lordship over themselves?

If this most honorable creature, one endowed with the widest scope of free will, has so little part in its own ownership and lordship, to what degree can other animate and lifeless things claim lordship over themselves?

O Europe! You have fallen into such error because your genius has caused you to forget your Lord—the Creator of everything. As a result, this illusion about your true nature has caused you to attribute all things and acts to (material) causes, and to share what belongs to God with false "claimants" to divinity. This compels all living beings to struggle with innumerable aversions and hostilities to satisfy their endless needs through an atom's weight of power, the capacity of will of a strand of hair, a single gleam's light of consciousness, and a tiny sparkle of life. Whatever they have (in the name of power and will, consciousness and life) cannot satisfy even one of their needs. When misfortune visits them, they seek help from deaf and blind causes. *But the appeals of unbelievers are but destined to go to waste* (13:14).

Your dark and darkening genius has changed humanity's day into a night illuminated by false, illusory lights. Those lights do not smile with joy in the face of humankind rather they mock their idiotic rejoicings in their pitiful and lamentable state.

Students of your genius see every living being as a wretched one attacked by darkness from all sides. They see the world as an abode of lamentation, and all voices in it are wailings over death and suffering. Students completely educated by your genius become pharaohs and tyrants, but such pharaohs and tyrants that they adore the meanest things and are attached to every beneficial means as if these means were their lords. They are apparently refractory, but so humble themselves for the sake of pleasures that they even kiss Satan's feet for the meanest benefit. They appear to be very powerful, but as they have no point of support (in their inner worlds), they are in reality infinitely weak. Your students seek only to satisfy their carnal appetites, pursuing their own personal benefits under the screen of patriotism and self-sacrifice, and working to satisfy their greed and conceit. They love only their own self and sacrifice everything for it.

The sincere students of the Qur'an, however, are worshipping servants of God, but they are such esteemed servants that they do not lower themselves even before the greatest creature or interest, and do not make even the supreme benefit of Paradise the aim of their worship. They are mild and gentle, but only humble themselves before their Creator and with His permission, and they exert themselves for the well-being of all humanity in both worlds. They are poor, but independent of all through what their Munificent Lord has stored in them; they are weak, but the strongest of all through their Master's strength, Whose power is infinite. Let alone seeking this fleeting world as their aim in life, they do not seek even to enter Paradise, and are not pleased with it. Would the Qur'an allow its true students to take this fleeting world as their aim in life while it does not allow them to take even eternal Paradise as their final goal? (Their aim is to obtain the good pleasure of their Lord alone, and Paradise is only a reward.) Thus you can understand what different aims these two kinds of students pursue in their efforts.

You can further compare the zeal and self-sacrifice of the students of the wise Qur'an with the pupils of your corrupt philosophy as follows:

The pupils of your corrupt philosophy flee from even their own family members to pursue their own interests, and even file a lawsuit against them. Whereas, the students of the Qur'an regard all righteous inhabitants of the heavens and earth as family members, and feel so strong and sincere a relationship with them that they pray for them, saying, "O God, forgive all believing men and women!" Their happiness makes the Qur'an's students happy. They see even the greatest things, such as the Supreme Throne of God and the sun, as God's dutiful and subjugated officials and as servants and creatures like themselves.

The Qur'an imparts such joy and elation to the spirits of its students that in place of the string of ninety-nine prayer beads, it gives all the atoms of the ninety-nine worlds that display the manifestations of the ninety-nine Divine Names to its students as prayer beads. It says to them, "Recite your glorifications and supplications with these!" Look at such saintly students of the Qur'an as 'Abdul-Qadir al-Jilani, ar-Rufa'i,[24] and

---

[24] Ahmad ibn 'Ali ibn Yahya ar-Rufa'i (1120–1184), founder of the Rufa'iya Sufi order, is one of the most renowned and celebrated saints of Islam. (Tr.)

ash-Shadhili,[25] and see how they used everything in the universe, down to the chains of atoms, raindrops, and breaths of all creatures to glorify, mention, and praise God.

Thus, look at the miraculous instruction of the Qur'an of miraculous exposition and see how humans are elevated by it—although defeated by a microbe and driven to distress and despair by the least grief and anxiety, see to what exalted ranks they rise, to what extent their faculties are developed by the Qur'an's enlightening guidance. Such people regard the world and its contents as insufficient to say their beads, for their daily recitations, and they belittle Paradise as the aim of their invocations, glorifications, and praises. Despite this, they do not consider themselves greater or more virtuous than the least of God's creatures. They combine the utmost dignity with the utmost modesty and humility. You can see from this how abject the students of corrupt philosophy are.

So, concerning the truths which the one-eyed genius of corrupt Western philosophy perceives wrongly, the guidance of the Qur'an—which considers the two worlds, which looks at them with its two shining eyes, penetrating the Unseen, and points with its two hands to the happiness of humankind in both worlds—says:

> O humanity! The selfhood and property which you hold in your hand is not yours; it is in trust to you. It belongs to the Owner (of all things); He is an All-Compassionate and All-Munificent One, Who has power over and knows everything. He wants to buy from you His property that He entrusted to you, to preserve it on your behalf so that you will not lose it. He will give you a very great price in return. Like a soldier, you have responsibilities and certain duties, so act in His Name and for His sake. He provides you with whatever you need and protects you against whatever you cannot overcome.
>
> The purpose of your life is to reflect the manifestations of His Names and Essential Qualities. When misfortune visits, you say, "*Surely we are God's and in His service, and surely to Him we are bound to return* (2: 156). So, O misfortune, if you have come with His permission, welcome. We are returning unto Him and desire a vision of Him. He will free us from life's duties and difficulties whenever He wills. If, O misfortune, this is to happen through your hand, it

---

[25] Shaykh Hasan ash-Shadhili (d. 1258): One of the leading, most celebrated saints of Islam. He founded the Shadhiliyah, one of the most important Sufi brotherhoods. (Tr.)

is alright. However, if He has allowed you to come to test my truthfulness to His trust, but has not allowed me to submit myself to you, so long as I have the power I will never submit His trust to one not entitled to receive it."

This is one of the numerous examples of being able to see the reality of the two ways. But people vary in guidance and misguidance, and heedlessness has many degrees. Everyone cannot perceive completely this truth in all its degrees. For heedlessness numbs the senses. Especially in the present age, it has numbed the senses to such an extent that the "civilized" are insensible to this acute pain. However, increased sensitivity owing to developments in the sciences, and the warnings of tens of thousands of deaths every day may yet tear this veil of heedlessness asunder. But how regrettable it is that many people in Muslim lands imitate Westerners blindly and take the way of misguidance under the influence of their irreligious trends of thought and scientific materialism.

O young people, especially those in Muslim lands! Do not try to imitate Westerners blindly! After you have suffered such misfortune at the hands of this second Europe, how can you still trust in and follow its debauched fallacies? Those who imitate them in their dissipation join their ranks unconsciously and condemn to death both themselves and their brothers and sisters. Be aware that the more you follow them in immorality, the more you contradict your claims of patriotism! Does your following them in this way mean despising devotion to "national" values and ridiculing the nation? May God guide us, and you, to the Straight Path.

The Twenty-Fourth Gleam

Dress code for women

In the Name of God, the All-Merciful, the All-Compassionate.

O Prophet! Tell your wives and your daughters, as well as the women (wives and daughters) of the believers, to draw over themselves some part of their outer garments (when outside their homes and when before men whom they are not forbidden to marry because of blood relation). (33:59)

 HIS VERSE ORDERS THE VEILING OF WOMEN. HOWEVER, DISSOLUTE civilization opposes this order of the Qur'an; it does not consider the veiling of women to be natural for them, and regards it as a form of slavery.

The answer

I will explain only four of numerous instances of wisdom in this order of the wise Qur'an, which shows that veiling is entirely natural for women, and that any assertion contrary to it opposes the innate disposition of women.

THE FIRST INSTANCE OF WISDOM

Veiling is natural for women and their innate disposition demands it. For women are weak, gentle and delicate in nature, and feel in need of protection and help for both themselves and their children, whom they love more than their own lives. Therefore, they have an inborn tendency to make themselves loved and not to be rebuffed.

Also, six or seven out of every ten women are either advancing in age or unattractive. They do not want to show their age and be known to be unattractive. Many among them do not, out of jealousy, want to appear unattractive in relation to others who are more "beautiful." In addition, they are afraid of being subjected to aggression or aspersion, and do not want to be accused of unfaithfulness by their husbands. All these and similar other factors naturally lead them to cover themselves. If noted carefully, it is the elderly among women who hide themselves most. Out of ten women, there are only two or three who are both young and beautiful and do not feel uneasy about displaying themselves.

It is a fact that people are made uncomfortable at and hurt by the gaze of those whom they do not like, often finding it unbearable. Indeed, if a beautiful, immodestly dressed woman takes pleasure at the gaze of two or three out of the ten men who can canonically marry her, she cannot bear the gaze of the remaining seven or eight. Also, since a beautiful woman who is not morally corrupt is sensitive and easily affected, she will certainly be distressed at indecent, dirty looks that experiences have proven to have a harmful effect, and which are, indeed, poisonous. We even hear that in Europe, where women do not cover themselves, many women are disturbed by gazes and complain to the police, saying, "These scoundrels keep staring at us and disturb us." This means that the unveiling of women by modern civilization is contrary to their natures, while the order in the Qur'an for veiling is not only in conformity with women's natures, but it also saves these mines of compassion who may be worthy companions for all eternity from degeneration, abasement, and from what is, in effect, slavery and wretchedness.

Furthermore, women are by nature fearful of men who are strangers. Fear naturally demands protection. For in addition to having to bear the heavy burden of carrying a child for eight or nine months, which will certainly embitter eight or nine minutes' pleasure, there is also the possibility of suffering the calamity of bringing up the child for eight or nine years in return for the eight or nine minutes' illicit pleasure. As it frequently happens, a woman has a natural fear of men who are strangers, and her disposition causes her to keep away from them. Her natural weakness forces her not to stir up the appetites of strange men and cause their assault, showing that her cloak is her shield and stronghold. I was told that a shoe-shiner had beset the bare-legged wife of a high-ranking man in the capital city, in the market-place, in broad daylight in front of people. This deals a slap in the shameless faces of those who oppose the veiling of women.

THE SECOND INSTANCE OF WISDOM

The substantial and strong relationship, and the love and interest between men and women do not arise only from the needs of the worldly life. Indeed, a woman is not a companion of her husband only in the world; she is his companion also in the eternal life and he is hers. As she is so, she certainly should not attract the looks of others besides her husband, her everlasting companion, to her beauty, and should not offend him and arouse his jealousy. As, from belief, her believing husband's relationship with her is not restricted to this worldly life, he does not feel merely animal love towards her during her years while she has beauty, but rather he should both love and respect her sincerely not only when she is young and beautiful but also during her old age, as she will be his companion in also the other, eternal life; for sure, humanity requires that she should in return present her beauties to his view alone and restrict her love to him. Otherwise she would gain very little but lose much.

Islam demands that the husband and wife should be a good match each for the other. This should be so particularly in the matter of religion. How happy is the husband who sees his wife's good religious life and follows her, becoming a pious one in order not to lose her companionship in the eternal life. How happy is the wife who sees her husband's good religious life and becomes a pious, righteous one in order not to lose her eternal friend. Alas for the man who indulges in dissipation, which will lose him his righteous wife forever. How unfortunate is the woman who does not follow her God-revering, pious husband and loses her eternal, blessed friend. And thousands of woes on the unhappy husband and wife who imitate each other in transgression and dissipation, and help each other to enter Hellfire!

THE THIRD INSTANCE OF WISDOM

Happiness in family life is possible and continuous through mutual confidence, sincere respect, and love between the husband and wife. Immodest dress and indecency destroy this mutual confidence, respect, and love. For many out of the women who prefer immodest dress wish to be found beautiful and attractive by others. (Most husbands think that their wives who prefer immodest dress want to make themselves loved by other men whom they find more handsome than them.) There can always be men who are more handsome than the husband of any wife. Nine out of ten of them will find men who are more handsome than their husbands. And only one out of twenty men does not find women who are more beautiful than his wife. Then, in addition to the evaporation of the mutual love and respect between the couples, extremely ugly and base feelings may arise, as follows:

By nature, men do not feel any lust towards the women who are within the forbidden degrees of relationship for marriage, like for example, their sisters, because the faces of such relatives suggest affection and licit love due to their close kinship, and thus do not arouse any sexual inclinations. But leaving uncovered the parts of the body which the Shari'a has forbidden to be exposed to close relatives, like the legs, might arouse extremely nasty feelings in some base souls. For the face of a close relative suggests close kinship and does not resemble the faces of others outside the degrees of kinship. However, a bare leg is the same as that of a canonical stranger in the feelings it may arouse. Since it does not have any distinguishing mark to recall the close kinship of its owner, it may attract lusty looks from some men of close kinship who have a low character. Such looks mean a degeneration that makes one's hair stand on end.

THE FOURTH INSTANCE OF WISDOM

Everyone wants to have children. There is no nation or government which does not support an increase in the population. In fact, the noblest Messenger, upon him be peace and blessings, declared, "Marry and increase, for on the Resurrection Day I will take pride in your large numbers in comparison to other communities."[26] However, immodest dress causes the number of marriages to decrease. For even the most dissolute and modern young man wants his wife to be chaste. Since he does not want her to be immodest like himself, he prefers remaining single, and even falls into illicit relationships.

Women cannot restrict their husbands' behavior to the extent that men can restrict theirs. For being the director of the internal affairs in the home, and therefore charged with all her husband's property, possessions, and children, the most essential characteristic of women is loyalty and confidence. Immodest dress may cause the husband to lose his confidence in her and suffer pangs of suspicion. In fact, courage and

---

[26] Abdur-Razzaq, *al-Musannaf*, 6:173; al-Ajluni, *Kashf al-Khafa'*, 1:380. (Tr.)

generosity, two praiseworthy qualities when found in men, are not regarded (in traditional communities) to be so in women as they are in men, as they may suggest a lack of trust and loyalty. The primary duties of men are to protect, provide maintenance, be kind, and respect, but the loyalty expected from women is greater. It is more difficult for women to restrict their husbands' behavior. While a woman cannot be shared and be married to more than one man at the same time, a man can have more than one woman in wedlock.

Our country cannot be compared with Europe because honor can be preserved there to a certain extent by violent means such as the duel, despite immodest dress. One who makes eyes at the wife of an honorable, self-respecting man does so only after he has taken his life in his own hand.[27] Furthermore, the people of Europe with the exception of those of the Mediterranean countries are mostly cold and frigid, like its climate. However, compared to Europe, the Muslim lands are torrid. It is a well-known fact that the environment has an effect on people's morality. In those cold countries, immodest dress excites the carnal appetites and desires of those cold people only relatively, and does not lead to much abuse. But immodest dress continually incites the carnal desires of the easily influenced and sensitive people of hot countries, and causes much abuse, waste, the weakening of young generations, and a loss of strength. Instead of satisfying natural needs once a month or every twenty days, people feel forced to do so every few days. Since they are obliged to avoid their wives for one to two weeks in every month because of contingencies like their monthly period, they are defeated by their carnal appetites, and will become inclined to illicit relationships.

Urban people cannot attempt to unveil women on the pretext of how rural women dress. For rural women have to work outside and do heavy work for the livelihood of themselves and their families, which usually makes them worn-out and somewhat coarse. Therefore, their being partially unveiled neither attracts as much attention like urban women nor incites carnal desires. Furthermore, since there are also only a few dissolute, idle men in villages, even one tenth of the vice witnessed in cities is not found there. So such a comparison cannot be made.

---

[27] This was so historically. (Tr.)

The First Letter

Figurative love and true love

In the Name of God, the All-Merciful, the All-Compassionate.

QUESTION:
Love for the opposite sex, called "figurative love" by Muslim saints and scholars, sometimes can become true or real love (love for the Creator). Can this happen with the love of the world?

ANSWER: The world has two faces; one mortal and transient, the other a mirror in which Divine Names are manifested and which is a field sown with seeds for the next life. If its lovers can turn away from its transient face to the other, such a love can change into love of God. But such lovers should not take their own particular, small, and perishable world for the whole vast outer world. If they forget themselves, become immersed in and fall in love with the external world, they, along with the misguided, will drown in the bog of nature worship—unless a hand miraculously comes to their aid.

Consider this analogy: Four of us are in a room with four walls, and each wall has a full-length mirror. This makes at least five rooms appear: one real and common to all of us, and "private" rooms reflected in each of our mirrors. Each of us can change our private room's shape, appearance, and color by manipulating our own mirror. For example, we can make it green or red, by painting the mirror, or give it different shapes. But we cannot change the shared real room so easily. Although both private and common rooms appear to be almost identical, their disposition and manageability is quite different. You can destroy your reflected, private room with a finger, whereas you cannot even move a stone of the shared real one.

Likewise, the world is a decorated station in which each person's life is a full-length mirror. In this station, each of us has a private world of which the pillar, center, or gate is our own life. Our private world can be compared to a page on which our deeds are recorded with the pen of our life. We love our private world, but inevitably realize that this world is built around our life and so, like our life, is transient, unstable, and perishable.

Given this, we should give our heart to the Divine Names' manifestations and not to perishable things. Furthermore, we should know that our private world is assigned to us as a field in which to plant seeds to grow into our Paradise, and that we should love it for the sake of the fruits we will harvest in the other world. If we devote our love to the fruits of our deeds and the Divine manifestations, our love for the world will change into love for God. Otherwise, as stated in: *Be not as those who forgot God, and so He caused them to forget themselves; they are the ungodly* (59:19), we might drown in our private world by forgetting ourselves and our private world's temporary nature, and so embrace our worldly life as if we and it would last forever.

Such a love for the world's transient face causes endless pain and suffering, for it engenders a pathetic compassion and despairing tender-heartedness. Sensitive lovers feel pity for all beings and, accordingly, their feelings are wounded by the perishing of all beautiful, mortal creatures. As they can do nothing for them, they suffer great hopelessness.

On the other hand, those who find God discover a remedy for the ailments caused by such feelings of compassion and tender-heartedness. Perceiving that the souls of all living beings, for whose perishing they feel such pity, are mirrors in which a Permanent Being's permanent Names are reflected constantly, their tender-heartedness changes into accepting joy and ease of mind. They understand that behind all the beautiful (but mortal and perishable) creatures is a pure grace and a sacred beauty manifested permanently through their delicate workmanship, ornamentation, and the wonder with which they are favored and illumined.

And so they understand how death and perishing are only processes of renewal to refresh and augment the beauty and pleasures and also to display the Divine artistry observed in the universe. Their pleasure in and appreciation of all Divine manifestations increases, as does their ardor.

The Everlasting: He is the Everlasting.

The Ninth Letter

Orientation of human feelings and inclinations, and iman (belief–conviction) and islam (Muslimness)

In the Name of God, the All-Merciful, the All-Compassionate.

HOSE WHO REGARD THIS WORLD AS A MILITARY GUEST-HOUSE AND live accordingly are the happiest of all people. They can rise to the rank of being approved and loved by God Almighty, the highest spiritual rank, and do not sell something of the greatest value for almost nothing. Such people live happy lives on the Straight Path and do not deviate.

Worldly affairs and things are almost as worthless and brittle as glass, while those belonging to the Hereafter are as valuable as diamonds and impossible to break. All human instincts, such as curiosity and love, passion and desire, are implanted in people to help them earn a happy life in the Hereafter. If one exploits them for the sake of this life, they only buy brittle glass at the price of diamonds.

On this subject, I would like to emphasize one point: Love is a very strong emotion. Feeling it for mortal beings either throws lovers into endless pain and sorrow or, since mortal beings are not worth so sincere a love, leads lovers toward seeking the Permanent Beloved One. In the latter case, it becomes real love.

Each of a person's thousands of feelings has two aspects: figurative and real. For example, everyone worries about the future even though they have no guarantee that they will be alive tomorrow. Then, they realize that they will die only at their appointed time. As a result, they stop worrying about their uncertain future here and focus on their eternal future beginning with death. That is a future worth worrying about, especially for those who do not heed the Divine commandments.

In the same way, people feel great passion for wealth and position. But they soon understand that wealth, fame, and position are not worth it, for such things may remove their dignity, reveal such degrading attitudes as show and hypocrisy, or cause them to bow and humble themselves before others. But above all, these things are temporary. In the end, such people incline toward the spiritual ranks and nearness to God and busy themselves with good deeds so that they will have provisions for their eternal life. Their inordinate ambition to acquire transient things thus changes into acquiring what is eternal.

People's excessive inclination toward insignificant, transient things can be obstinate. But if they eventually realize that this obstinate attachment is of no benefit, such obstinacy can become persistence for belief's truths or Islam's fundamentals, as well as for striving for the next life.

If people exploit their spiritual faculties to satisfy their sensual and worldly desires and live in this world as if they will stay here forever, those faculties will lead to immoral qualities and cause much waste. But if people use them to prosper in the Hereafter, without neglecting life's essential needs, these faculties will lead to laudable moral qualities and happiness in either world in accordance with wisdom and truth.

One reason why preachers' advice is ineffective nowadays is that they invite people to change their nature. They advise: "Do not be envious or ambitious, do not feel enmity or be obstinate, do not love the world," and so on. Such advice is useless, for it is against human nature. Instead, these energies can and should be channeled into good deeds and directed toward positive aims. For example, love for the world can be channeled into love for the other world, enmity can be directed against one's carnal self, and envy can become a means for competing to do good deeds.

Muslim scholars have discussed at length whether *islam* (being a Muslim) and *iman* (belief–conviction) are different. Some say they are the same and others say they are different, although one is not acceptable without the other. I see a difference between them, as follows: *Islam* is choosing a side, while *iman* means affirming with certainty.

In other words, *islam*, or being a Muslim, means siding with, submitting to, and obeying the truth. *Iman*, or being a believer (*mu'min*), means confirming and confessing the truth of Islam. I know some people who strongly advocate the Qur'an's commandments even though they are not believers. Such people may be considered *muslim* in the literal sense (of those who surrender) because they observe some of Islam's elements without believing in all of them. Some believers cannot be considered *muslim*, for they do not pay much attention to the Qur'an's commandments or try to obey them.

Question: Is belief without *islam* or being a Muslim—without obedience and practice in daily life—enough for one to prosper in the other world?

Answer: Those who live according to the Qur'an's commandments but without belief, and believers who do not apply the Divine commandments in their lives, will not prosper in the other world. The proofs of Islam, as numerous as all particles in creation and as strong as the chain of beings, and the truths of the Qur'an and belief are expounded so clearly in the *Risale-i Nur* that they provide the reader with firm belief and submission.

Whenever I recite in the daily rite of Shah Naqshband, after confessing my belief: "We live with this confession, and we die with it, and tomorrow we will be resurrected with it," I feel that I would not give up even one truth of belief, even if the whole world were offered to me. It is unbearable for me to think any thought contrary to one truth of belief, even for a second. If the whole world were my private property, even my carnal self would not oppose sacrificing it in return for establishing one truth of belief.

I feel a very firm belief in my heart when I recite: "We believe in all the Prophets You raised up, and we believe in all the Scriptures You sent down, and we confirm them all." I consider it impossible to think or believe otherwise, and consider misguided people as infinitely stupid and foolish.

I send my greetings and present my respects to your parents. I ask them to pray for me. They are like my own parents, as you are my brother in religion. I also send my greetings to everyone in your village, particularly to those who hear you read *The Words*.

The Everlasting: He is the Everlasting.

The Twenty-ninth Letter

God is the Light of the heavens and the earth

In the Name of God, the All-Merciful, the All-Compassionate.

God is the Light of the heavens and the earth. (24:35)

URING THE HOLY MONTH OF RAMADAN, I EXPERIENCED ONE OF THE numerous radiances of mystery of the light-diffusing verse: *God is the Light of the heavens and the earth*. My heart was convinced that all living creatures make the same supplication to God, such as that of Uways al-Qarani:

> O God, You are my Lord and I am Your servant;
> You are the Creator and I am the one created;
> You are the All-Providing and I am the one provided...

and I felt that each of the 18,000 worlds receives its light from one Divine Name.

The world may be likened to a multipetalled rose-bud consisting of many kinds of worlds wrapped up within each other. I saw a new one behind or under each one's veil. Each world manifested itself to me in darkness and frightening gloom, as depicted by:

> *Or like the veils of darkness in a vast deep ocean, overwhelmed by a great wave topped by a great wave, topped by dark clouds, one darkness over another, such that if a man stretches out his hand he can hardly see it. For whomsoever God has not appointed light, for him there is no light.* (24:40)

In my vision, a Divine Name suddenly manifested and enlightened each world appearing to me in darkness because of heedlessness. This journey of the heart or the imagination lasted for a long time. What follows is a summary:

The animal world appeared very gloomy, for animals are impotent and weak, have innumerable needs, and suffer severe hunger. But the Divine Name the All-Merciful suddenly appeared like a shining sun above the tower of the All-Provider and thoroughly illuminated that world with the light of Mercy.

After that, I saw within that world another pitiful one in which the young desperately struggle in impotent need. Suddenly the Name the All-Compassionate rose above the tower of the All-Caring and so beautifully illuminated that world that it changed tears of sorrow into tears of joy, happiness, and the pleasure of thanksgiving.

Then the human world manifested itself, as if on a screen. It was so dark, gloomy, and terrifying that I was filled with panic and exclaimed: "How pitiful!" I saw that people have infinite desires and ambitions, universal ideas and imaginations, and grand inclinations and dispositions to eternity and eternal happiness in Paradise. Nevertheless, in addition to their infinite weakness, impotence, and need, they are exposed to innumerable misfortunes and hostile attacks. They flow, either singly or in groups, through a short tumultuous life, a miserable livelihood, and under the tragic blows of continual decay and separation. When they finally reach the grave, which (to the heedless) appears as a gate opening onto eternal darkness, they are hurled into a dark pit. I almost collapsed in tears, with all my senses and my intellect, heart, and soul, at the sight of such a pitifully dark and gloomy world.

But then the Divine Name the All-Just was manifested in the meaning of the All-Wise, along with the Name the All-Merciful in the meaning of the All-Munificent, the Name the All-Compassionate in the meaning of the All-Forgiver, the Name the Raiser of the Dead in the meaning of the Heir-to-All, the Name the Reviver in the meaning of the All-Beneficent, and the Name the Lord in the meaning of the Master. Those Names illuminated many spheres within that dark human world and, opening windows on them from the luminous World of the Hereafter, diffused light upon it.

Afterwards, another huge screen displayed the earth and its contents. The obscure laws of science and the principles of corrupt philosophy showed it as terrifying and gloomy. The miserable condition of humanity, floating in infinite space on the old earth in a state of continuous volcanic eruption inside and apt to disintegration, moving at such a great speed as to revolve around the sun in a year, seemed frighteningly gloomy. I was dazed and felt dizzy.

But all at once, the Names the Creator of the universe and the earth, the All-Powerful, All-Knowing, Lord, God, Lord of the heavens and the earth, and Subduer of the sun and the moon appeared in the manifestation of Mercy, Grandeur, and Lordship. They so illumined that world that I saw it as a safe, perfect, and beautiful ship subjected to humanity so that people could travel for pleasure or business.

In sum, I saw that each of the 1,001 Divine Names is like a sun illuminating one of those worlds. Each one contains many spheres, and all other Names manifest themselves in some degree of ordered relation to that Name's full manifestation due to God's Oneness.

Discerning a different light behind each veil of darkness, my heart wanted to mount on the imangination and make a journey upward to the world of the heavens. I saw that those radiant planets, which appear to be smiling, are bigger than the earth and revolve faster than it. If even one of them became confused, it would collide with another and destroy the universe. So I saw the heavens as a dark, boundless, and frightening space, with the moving or fixed stars radiating fire and light. I regretted coming here.

But then the Divine Beautiful Names the Lord of the heavens and the earth and the Lord of the angels and the spirit manifested themselves and disclosed the meaning of: *We have adorned the nearest heaven with lamps* (67:5) and: *He has subdued the sun and the moon* (13:2). Each star, located in darkness, received a gleam from those Names' mighty light, and the heavens were illuminated as if as many lamps as the stars had been lit. That space, formerly imagined to be dark and empty, was thronged and animated and brightened by angels and spirit beings. The suns and stars, serving as a host of the King of eternity, seemed to demonstrate, as if performing an exalted maneuver, the Majestic King's magnificence and His Lordship's splendor. If I had had enough strength, if my bodily particles would have obeyed me, and if I could have done so in all creatures' languages, I would have recited:

> *God is the light of the heavens and the earth. The parable of His Light is as if there were a niche and within it a lamp, the lamp enclosed in glass, the glass as it were a brilliant star, lit from a blessed tree, an olive, neither of the east nor of the west, whose oil would almost glow forth of itself*

though no fire touched it. Light upon light! God guides to His Light whom
He wills. (24:35)

However, I recited that verse on behalf of all creatures and, awakening, returned to the earth saying: "All praise be to God for the light of belief and the Qur'an."

The Eleventh Ray

Some of belief's fruits

In the Name of God, the All-Merciful, the All-Compassionate.

A Summary of the second matter

AS EXPLAINED IN THE TREATISE ENTITLED GENÇLIK REHBERI ("A Guide for Youth") in the *Risale-i Nur*, death is as inevitable as night following day, or winter following fall. Just as this prison is a temporary guesthouse for those who enter and leave it one after the other, the earth too is a like a caravanserai on a long road; here caravans, rushing to get to their destination, stay overnight before moving on. Surely death, which has emptied all of the cities of the earth into the bowels of the earth a hundred times over, places demands on us far greater than those demanded by life. The *Risale-i Nur* has explained this awesome truth, a brief summary of which follows:

Since death cannot be eliminated and since the door of the grave cannot be closed, we must look for a way that can save us from being condemned by the executioner of death to the solitary confinement of the grave and eternal perdition in the world to come; surely this should be humankind's greatest concern and surely it is in our best interest to investigate this possibility? There is such a way—a way shown by *Risale-i Nur* and inspired by the teachings of the Qur'an. What follows is a brief summary:

Death is either eternal execution—a gallows on which a person and their friends and relatives will be hanged—or it is a kind of entrance ticket to another, permanent realm, a palace of happiness prepared for those who possess belief. As for the grave, it is either a dark, bottomless pit of solitary confinement or a door which opens outward from the prison of this world onto a permanent, illuminated garden and place of feasting. This truth has been expounded in the *Gençlik Rehberi* as follows:

For example: many gallows have been set up in this prison yard, and immediately beyond the wall a huge lottery office has been opened; everyone in the world has purchased a ticket. There is no doubt whatsoever that the five hundred people in this prison are certain to be called one by one, without exception, to that yard: there is no hope of escape. One can hear the announcements being made: "Come and receive your document of execution and mount the gallows!" or "Take in your hand the decree condemning you to eternal solitary confinement and enter through that door!" or "Congratulations! Yours is the winning ticket that is worth millions. Come and take it!" We see with our own eyes that people are mounting the gallows, one after the other. Yet, while some mount the gallows only to be hanged, we learn from the reports of the earnest officials who are working in the prison yard that some of the people are using the gallows as one would a ladder, and are scaling the wall to enter the lottery office that lies beyond.

At this juncture, two delegations enter our prison. One delegation brings musical instruments, wine and apparently delicious sweetmeats and pastries, which they endeavor to make us eat. But the sweetmeats are in fact poisonous, for demons in human form have put poison in them.

The second delegation brings papers of education and training, lawful foods and licit drinks. The members of this delegation present these things to us and say with great earnestness:

"The gifts brought by the first delegation are a test; if you accept and consume them, you will be hanged on the gallows over there, like the others that you have seen hanged before them. However, if you accept the gifts that we have brought you at the command of this country's ruler, and if you recite the supplications and prayers written on these papers of education and training, you will be saved from execution. Believe without a shadow of a doubt that each of you will receive the winning lottery ticket worth millions as a royal favor. But if you eat these unlawful, poisonous sweets, it is written in these decrees—decrees with which we all concur—that you will suffer the effects of the poison until the very moment that you are taken to the gallows to be hanged."

As in this comparison, for the people of belief and obedience—provided that they depart in a state of true belief—the ticket for an eternal and inexhaustible treasury will be drawn from the lottery of human fate beyond the gallows at the appointed hour, of which we are always aware. However, for those with no belief in the Hereafter and who persist in vice, unlawful actions, unbelief and sin, there is a hundred per cent probability that they will, unless they repent, be condemned by judicial decree to execution and eternal perdition. For those who believe in the immortality of the human spirit, yet still tread the path of vice and sin there is a ninety-nine per cent probability that they will be condemned to permanent solitary confinement. Certain news of this was given by one hundred and twenty-four thousand Prophets, all of whom were equipped with innumerable miracles as evidence of their truthfulness. The same news has been given by more than one hundred and twenty-four million saints, who discern and affirm through spiritual uncovering the traces and shadows—as though seen on a movie screen—of the news brought by the Prophets. Similarly, thousands of millions of exacting scholars, interpreters of the Islamic law and veracious scholars have, with decisive proofs and powerful arguments, established with rational and logical certainty the information provided by these two eminent groups of people.

Consider, then, the situation of someone who, on the advice of a single individual, abandons the safe path they have been following and opts for a longer and much more dangerous one, ignoring the collective wisdom of the people of truth mentioned earlier—those moons, suns and stars, those sacred leaders of humanity—who have pointed out the straight path which leads directly to eternal felicity.

The situation of such a person is this: having embarked on this journey, the wretch hears someone say that by taking the short path there is a one per-cent chance of danger and the possibility of a month's incarceration at the end of the road. So, on the spurious advice of a single person, our traveler abandons the short path and takes a longer route. They do this because it appears harmless, although in reality there is no benefit in this path. At the same time, innumerable wise and well-informed individuals warn them not to abandon the shorter and easier of the routes—the one which will, with utmost certainty, lead them eventually to Paradise and eternal happiness. However, they chose to ignore their words and opt for the rougher, more troublesome route—the one which, with ninety-nine percent certainty, will lead to incarceration in Hell and everlasting misery. Surely, such a wretch has lost their mind, their heart and their spirit, for only a drunken lunatic would flee from the slight sting of a few mosquitoes on the safe path and rush onto a route along which dragons hide, waiting to attack and tear the poor wretch limb from limb.

Since this is the reality of the situation, we prisoners should accept the gifts of the second, blessed delegation so that we may avenge ourselves completely for the calamity of our incarceration. That is to say, just as the pleasure of a minute's revenge or a few minutes of vice has condemned us to years of incarceration, making our worlds into a prison, in order to take revenge we should transform an hour or two of our prison lives into a day or two of worship. In this way we will be able to transform two or three-year sentences into twenty or thirty years of permanent life thanks to the gifts of that blessed delegation; in this way we will be able to turn prison sentences of twenty or thirty years into a means of forgiveness from millions of years of incarceration in Hell, thus allowing our everlasting lives to smile in retaliation for the weeping that has characterized our transitory worlds. Demonstrating that prison is a place of training and education, we should try to be well-behaved, trustworthy, and useful members of our nation and country. Prison officers, wardens, and administrators should also see that the men whom they considered to be bandits, vagrants, murderers, and men of vice—and thus harmful to the country—are in fact students engaged in study in this most blessed place of education. And they should feel pride and offer thanks to God for this bounty.

The third matter

What follows is a summary of an instructive incident that is described in Gençlik Rehberi:

I was once sitting by a window in Eskişehir Prison during the National Republic Day. The young girls in the school opposite the prison were playing and cheering in the schoolyard. Suddenly, I saw them fifty years on, their future conditions played out to me like a film on a movie screen. I saw that of those fifty to sixty girl students, forty to fifty had turned to dust in their graves and were suffering. The other ten were unattractive septuagenarians, despised by those from whom they might have expected love, on account of the fact that they had not preserved their chastity when young. Observing this, I wept at their pitiable states. Some of my friends in the prison heard my weeping and asked me what was wrong, but I had to tell them to leave me alone for a while.

You must understand that what I saw was real and not imaginary. Just as summer and fall are followed by winter, the summer of youth and the fall of old age are followed by the winter of the grave and the Intermediate

Realm. If there were a device which could show future events in the same way that films can show the events of the past, then those of fifty years ago would be shown in the present, and the people of misguidance and vice would be shown their condition fifty years from now; they would cry out in pain and disgust, bemoaning bitterly their present state of apparent felicity and illicit pleasures.

While preoccupied with these observations in Eskişehir Prison, a sort of collective persona, which encourages vice and misguidance, appeared embodied before me like a devil in human form. It said:

"We want to taste all the pleasures and joys of life, and to make others taste them too; do not interfere with us!"

In response I said:

"Since for the sake of pleasure and enjoyment you do not recall death but, rather, plunge yourself into vice and misguidance, know for a fact that because of your misguidance all the past is dead and non-existent: it is a desolate and most dreadful graveyard, filled with rotted corpses. The pains that arise from those innumerable separations you have suffered and from the deaths of your friends—pains which, since there is no hope of reunion with your loved ones, have had a grievous effect on what remains of your heart and mind—will soon destroy those insignificant drunken pleasures which constitute your present. As for the future, well, because of your lack of belief, that too is nothing more than a dark, dead, and desolate wasteland. And since the unfortunate wretches who are destined to come from there to emerge in this realm of existence and in the present will also be beheaded by the executioner's sword of death and, according to your assumption, thrown into non-existence, on account of your concern and relationship with them which stems from your being a creature with intelligence, grievous worries will rain down continuously on your disbelieving head, devastating beyond recognition your petty, dissolute pleasure.

"If you abandon misguidance and vice and enter the sphere of true belief and righteousness, you will see through the light of faith that the past is neither non-existent nor a graveyard filled with rotted corpses; rather, it is a real, luminous world that has been transformed into the future: it is a waiting-room for the immortal spirits who will enter palaces of happiness in the world to come. Since it is so, it gives no pain; on the contrary, depending on the degree and strength of one's belief, it causes a sort of paradisiacal pleasure in the world. The future, too, when seen through the eye of belief, is not a dark, desolate wasteland, but a ground in whose palaces of eternal happiness banquets and exhibitions of gifts have been set up by an All-Merciful, All-Compassionate One of Majesty and Benevolence—One Who has infinite Mercy and Munificence and Who makes spring and summer into tables laden with bounties. Since the movie screen of belief reveals the future to be like this and since belief also gives the awareness that people are being dispatched there through the door death, everyone can experience some sort of the pleasure pertaining to that permanent realm while still in this world, to the degree and strength of their belief. *In conclusion, true, pain-free pleasure can be found only in belief and is possible only through belief.*

"Since it is related to our discussion, we will explain something which was included in *Gençlik Rehberi* as a postscript, namely a single instance of the thousands of benefits and pleasures that belief produces even in this world. It is as follows:

"Imagine, for example, that your beloved only child is suffering the pangs of death and you are desperately worried about her painful demise. Suddenly, a physician like Khidr or Luqman appears with a wonderful medicine, which he gives to your loved one. Your dear, most adorable child opens her eyes, delivered from death. Can you imagine the joy and relief that you would feel at her recovery and escape from death?

"Like the child in the example, countless people whom you love and for whom you are concerned are, in your view, about to rot away for all eternity in the graveyard of the past. Suddenly, like Luqman the Wise, the truth of belief shines a light from the window of the heart onto the grave, which is thought of as a vast place of eternal annihilation. Thanks to the truth and light of belief, all of the dead spring to life, as though saying, 'We did not die and will not die; we will meet with you again!' What boundless joy and exhilaration you would feel at experiencing this reality! By giving the same boundless joy and exhilaration in this world, belief proves that it is like a seed—a seed which, were it to be embodied, would grow into a private paradise, a veritable *Touba*-tree of eternal felicity."

Persisting in its obduracy, that devil in human form responded thus:

"At least we can pass our lives like animals, immersed in pleasure and enjoyment, indulging ourselves with amusement and dissipation, and casting all thought of these subtle and delicate matters out of our minds!"

My answer was as follows:

"No, you cannot live like an animal, not least because neither past nor future exists for animals. They feel neither sorrow nor regret over the past nor worry or fear with regard to what is yet to come. An animal receives unalloyed pleasure. It lives and sleeps in comfort, offering thanks and praise to its Creator. Even an animal that is about to be slaughtered does not feel anything. It feels pain as the knife cuts its throat, but that pain is momentary and disappears in an instant. This means that keeping the Unseen unknown, without revealing what will happen there, is a great instance of Divine mercy and compassion; it is an even greater blessing for innocent animals. But on account of the fact that human beings are sentient, and because their past and future can be seen to emerge from the Unseen to some extent, what lies beyond the veil of the visible world cannot remain wholly hidden; as a result, O human being, you are unable to live as carefree and unconcerned as animals. Regrets about the past, the pain of separation and worries about the future reduce to ashes your fleeting present pleasures, making them a hundred times less appealing than those enjoyed by the animals. Since this is a fact, either abandon your intellect, turn yourself into an animal, and achieve salvation that way or, alternatively, come to your senses through true belief, pay heed to the Qur'an, and experience pure pleasure also in this transitory world, which is a hundred times greater than that enjoyed by animals."

For a while, these words of mine silenced my adversary. But in his obstinacy he turned to me once more and said: "Well, then, we can at least live like the irreligious people of the West."

I replied:

"In the same way that you cannot live like animals, you cannot live like the irreligious people of the West either. For even if they deny one Prophet, they believe in others. Even if they do not recognize the Prophets, they may believe in God. And even if they do not know God, they may have certain personal characteristics and virtues through which they find fulfillment. But if a Muslim denies the final Prophet, the greatest of God's Messengers, upon him and them be peace and blessings, whose religion and mission are universal, to what can they turn? For they will be unable to accept any other Prophet and will even have to turn their back on God Himself. For their knowledge of God and all the other Prophets has reached them through Prophet Muhammad, upon him be peace and blessings; without him, how can other Prophets have a place in anyone's heart?

It is because of this that while many people have, since the earliest times, abandoned other faiths to enter Islam, few, if any, Muslims have become true Jews or Christians. Muslims who abandon Islam tend rather to become completely irreligious: as a rule, their characters are corrupted and they become a danger to the country and nation."

Hearing this argument, the obstinate devil in human garb could find no further straw at which to clutch. Unable to respond, it disappeared and went to Hell.

So, classmates of mine in this School of Joseph! Reality is as I have described it, affirmed by the *Risale-i Nur* which, with its proofs, has worn down the obduracy of many an obstinate soul and caused numerous people to believe over the past twenty years. Since it is thus, we should therefore follow the way of belief and correct conduct—a way which is safe and easy, and which benefits our lives and those of the members of our nation not only in this world but also in the next. Instead of indulging ourselves with pointless and ultimately painful fantasies, we should spend our free time reciting the *suras* of the Qur'an that we have memorized and learn their meaning from friends who can teach them. We should make up for the canonical Prayers we have failed to perform in the past. And, taking advantage of each other's good qualities, we should try to transform this prison into a blessed garden in which the seeds of good character can be nurtured. With righteous deeds such as these, we should do our best so that the prison governor and those concerned may be kindly masters and guides charged with the duty of preparing people for Paradise in the School of Joseph and supervising their training and education, rather than dispensers of torment, like the Angels of Hell, who stand over criminals and murderers.

The fourth matter

Again, this matter has been explained in *Gençlik Rehberi*. I was once asked the following question by some brothers who were helping me:

"For fifty days now you have asked nothing at all, nor have you shown any curiosity, about this terrible World War which has thrown the whole world into chaos, even though it is connected closely with the fate of Islam and the Muslim World. However, some of the religious and the learned listen to the radio intently, and some are even distracted from congregational Prayers as a result. Is there some other event more momentous than this war? Or is it in some way harmful to be preoccupied with it?"

My reply was as follows:

"The capital of life is very little and the work to be done very great. Like concentric circles, everyone has certain spheres of concern which exist one within the other: they have the spheres of the heart and the stomach; the spheres of body and home; the spheres of the quarter in which they reside and the town or city in which they live; the sphere of their country, the spheres of the earth and humankind, and the sphere of all living beings and the world as a whole. Each person may have certain duties in each of those spheres, but the most important and permanent duties are those which pertain to the nearest, smallest sphere, while the least important and temporary duties pertain to the furthest, largest one. According to this standard, there may be duties, the importance and sphere of which are inversely proportional to each other. But because of the appeal of the largest sphere, those vital duties that pertain to the smallest sphere tend to be neglected, as people become preoccupied with unnecessary, trivial, and peripheral matters. It destroys the capital of their life for nothing and causes them to waste their precious time on worthless things. For example, someone who follows the events of the war may come to support one side in their heart, and as result may even look favorably on tyranny and become a part of it.

"With regard to the first part of the question, all people—Muslims especially—are faced continuously with events more momentous than this World War, and an issue infinitely more important than that of world dominion. Indeed, if everyone had the wealth of the Germans and the English, plus an iota of sense, they would spend it all on finding a solution to this issue. This issue, about which hundreds of thousands of Prophets, saints, and purified scholars have informed us, relying on the thousands of promises and pledges given by the Owner and Disposer of the universe, is as follows:

"For everyone there exists the possibility of winning, thanks to belief, an eternal property that is as vast as the earth, filled with gardens and palaces. Without belief, however, that property cannot be gained. In this age, many are losing because of the plague of materialism. A certain saintly scholar, who was capable of unveiling certain hidden realities, once observed in one district that out of forty people who lay on their deathbeds, only a few won; the others lost. Can anything, even power and dominion over the whole world, substitute for such a loss?

"We *Risale-i Nur* students know that it would be foolhardy to abandon the duties conducive to felicity in the Hereafter, and to give up on that excellent lawyer who helps ninety-nine percent of the people to win their case, and instead preoccupy ourselves with trivia as though we would remain in this world forever. For this reason, we *Risale-i Nur* students are convinced that if each of us were a hundred times more intelligent than we are now, we would still use our intellectual capital on the same right cause.

"To my new brothers here who share with me the calamity of imprisonment I would say this. You have not yet come to know the *Risale-i Nur* as well as my old brothers, who entered this place with me. Calling on them and thousands of students like them as witnesses, I assure you that the *Risale-i Nur* is the leading 'lawyer' of the age, inspired by the miraculousness of the wise Qur'an and able to help those who study it to win the most important case of their lives. Indeed, over the past twenty years it has helped twenty thousand people to attain true belief—itself a guarantee that their case will be successful. Although for the past eighteen years my enemies and various heretics and materialists have cruelly turned some members of the government against me and the authorities have imprisoned us in order to silence us, something they have tried to do before, they have been able to criticize only two or three of the one hundred and thirty pieces of 'equipment' which make up the steel fortress of the *Risale-i Nur*. In other words, the *Risale-i Nur* is enough for one who wants to engage an advocate to win the case of their life. Also, do not fear, for the *Risale-i Nur* cannot be banned! With two or three exceptions, its most significant treatises are circulating freely among representatives and other leading figures of the government. By God's leave, a time will come when venerated governors and officials will distribute these lights to the prisoners as though they were food and medicine in order to turn the prisons into truly effective houses of reform."

A summary of the eighth matter

In this eghth matter I was planning to elucidate a hundredth of the benefits that belief in the Hereafter has for humanity and their felicity in both this world and the next. However, since the miraculous Qur'an leaves no need for further explanation concerning the benefits of belief in securing happiness in the Hereafter, and since the benefits of belief for humanity in this world have been discussed in detail in the *Risale-i Nur*, readers may refer to the Qur'an and the relevant sections of the *Risale-i Nur*. Here, we will summarize only three or four out of the hundreds of results of belief in the Hereafter concerning human individual and social life.

THE FIRST: Just as a person has relations with their home, they also have relations with the world beyond it. Similarly, just as they have relations with their relatives, they also have relations with the rest of humankind. And just as they desire a kind of temporary permanence in this world, they also yearn passionately for an enduring permanence in the realm of eternity. In the same way that a person strives to meet the need of their stomach for food, they are, by nature, compelled to strive to provide sustenance to the metaphorical stomachs of their mind, heart, spirit and humanity. Their desires and demands are such that nothing but eternity and everlasting felicity can satisfy them. As mentioned in The Tenth Word, when I was young I asked myself: "Do you want to live for a million years as ruler of the world but then be dispatched into eternal non-existence? Or would you prefer to have an ordinary and at times difficult existence, but live forever?" I saw that my imagination always opted for the latter, saying: "I want to live forever, even though it be in Hell!"

Thus, since the pleasures of this world do not satisfy the imaginative faculty, which is a servant of the human essence, it follows that the comprehensive essence of humanity is, by its very nature, attached to eternity. For despite being preoccupied with boundless hopes and desires, humanity has only an insignificant faculty of will as their capital, stricken as they are with absolute poverty. Belief in the Hereafter, then, is such a powerful and sufficient treasury, such a means of happiness and pleasure, such a refuge and source of assistance and benefit, and such a means of consolation in the face of the endless sorrows of this world that if the life of this world had to be sacrificed in order to gain it, it would still be a cheap price to pay.

ITS SECOND FRUIT AND BENEFIT PERTAINING TO HUMAN PERSONAL LIFE: This was explained in the third matter, and can be found in Gençlik Rehberi as a footnote.

The most constant and over-riding anxiety of humanity is that we will one day enter the grave, as our friends and relations have before us. The wretched human being, who is ready to sacrifice their very soul for a single friend, imagines that the countless millions of human beings who have entered the grave before them have been condemned to eternal annihilation, and this supposition makes them suffer the torments of Hell. Just at this point, belief in the Hereafter appears, opens our eyes and raises the veil. It tells us: "Look!" And looking with belief, we can see that our companions have been saved from eternal annihilation and are awaiting us happily in a light-filled world;

realizing this, we receive a spiritual pleasure that is a reflection of the pleasures of Paradise. Contenting ourselves with the explanations of this second fruit in the *Risale-i Nur*, we will curtail the discussion here.

A THIRD BENEFIT: Human beings are superior to other living beings on account of their elevated characteristics, their comprehensive abilities, their universal ability to worship and the extensive spheres of existence which make up their life. However, the virtues which characterize the human being, such as love, zeal, brother and sister-hood and humanity, are acquired in accordance with the extent of this fleeting present time, which is constricted between the past and the future, both of which are dark and non-existent.

For example, a person loves and serves their father, brother or sister, their spouse, nation or country, none of whom they knew before; they will see none of these people once they have departed from this world. Since the fleeting nature of life means that it is highly unlikely that a person would be able to achieve complete loyalty or sincerity in any one relationship, their virtues and excellences are proportionately diminished. Then, just at the point where they fall to a level lower than that of the animals and become more wretched than they already are because they have intellect and reason, belief in the Hereafter comes to this person's assistance. It expands the present, which is as narrow as the grave, to the extent that it encompasses the past and future and manifests a sphere of existence as broad as the world, stretching from pre-eternity to post-eternity. Realizing that relations with one's spouse, parents and siblings will continue for eternity in Paradise, they love, respect, help and have mercy on them while in this world. With this new realization, a person will not exploit such important duties based on the relationships that encompass this broad sphere of life and existence for the sake of the worthless affairs of this world and its petty interests. Being able to achieve earnest loyalty and sincerity, a person's good qualities and attainments begin to develop accordingly, and their humanity becomes exalted. While they cannot match even a sparrow in enjoyment of this life, they can become the noblest and happiest of guests in the universe, superior to all animals, as well as being the best loved and most appreciated servant of the universe's Owner. Since this matter has also been explained in the *Risale-i Nur*, we content ourselves here with this much.

A FOURTH BENEFIT OF BELIEF IN THE HEREAFTER, WHICH RELATES TO HUMAN SOCIAL LIFE: What follows is a summary of this benefit, expounded in the Ninth Ray of the *Risale-i Nur*:

Children, who make up a third of the human race, can live a truly human life and maintain truly human capacities only if they have sincere belief in the Hereafter. Without belief in the Hereafter, they are forced to compensate for the anxiety they feel over their eventual oblivion by filling their worldly life with trivia and meaningless distractions. For the constant deaths around them of children like themselves have such an effect on their sensitive minds and weak hearts, which cherish far-reaching desires, and vulnerable spirits, that it makes life torture for them and their reason a tool of suffering. If, however, they are brought to belief in the Hereafter, the anxieties they once felt at the deaths of their playmates, which they try to escape by immersing themselves in meaningless distractions, will give way to joy and exhilaration as they realize the truth. For supported by belief in the Hereafter they will say: "My sibling or playmate has died and become a bird in Paradise. He (or she) is now flying around and enjoying himself much more than we are. And although my mother has died, she has gone to the realm of Divine mercy. One day I will see her in Paradise, where she will take me into her arms once again." Such a realization will enable these children to live in a state which befits them as human beings.

It is only through believing in the Hereafter that the aged, who constitute another third of humankind, are able to find consolation in the face of what they see as the inevitable extinction of their lives and the fact that they too will soon be consigned to the bowels of the earth and their precious and lovable worlds have come to an end. Without belief in the Hereafter, those compassionate, respected fathers and those tender, self-sacrificing mothers would become so distraught and distressed in heart and spirit that their world would seem to be a prison of despair for them and life a heavy burden of torment. But belief in the Hereafter addresses them, saying: "Do not worry! A radiant, everlasting life awaits you and there you will enjoy eternal youth. You will be reunited in joy with your beloved children and the relatives that you have lost. All your good deeds have been preserved and you will be rewarded for them there." Belief in the Hereafter gives them such solace and joy that were they to experience old age a hundred times over, it would not cause them to despair.

A third of humankind is made up of the youth. With their turbulent passions and emotions and the difficulty they have in controlling their bold intellects if they lose their faith in the Hereafter and do not bring to mind the torments of Hell, the property and honor of the upright members of society, along with the peace and dignity of the weak and the elderly, will be at serious risk. One youth is able to bring down destruction on a happy home for the sake of one minute's pleasure, and the years of imprisonment that follow will turn them into a wild animal. But if belief in the Hereafter comes to their assistance, they quickly come to their senses, thinking: "It is true that the government informers do not see me and I can hide from them, but the angels of the All-Majestic Sovereign, Who has a prison known as Hell, see me and are recording all of my evil deeds. I am not free and left to my own devices: I am a traveler charged with duties. One day I too will be old and weak." Suddenly this person begins to feel sympathy and respect for those they would have assaulted before without thinking twice. Being content with the explanations of this truth which the reader may find in the *Risale-i Nur*, we cut the discussion short here.

Another important section of humankind comprises the sick, the oppressed, the poor, those like us who are disaster-stricken and prisoners languishing in jail, subject to severe punishment. If belief in the Hereafter does not come to their aid, their lives are bound to be filled with torment. For illness reminds them constantly of death; the haughty treachery of the oppressor, in the face of whom they are unable to save their honor, causes them extreme distress; the loss of property or offspring in serious disasters brings untold despair; and the intolerable hardship of having to spend five or ten years in prison causes immeasurable pain and mental suffering. Without belief, all of these calamitous situations turn the world into a terrible prison for those who experience them and life becomes a living hell. But if belief in the Hereafter comes to their aid, they begin to feel relief and, to the degree of their belief, their distress, despair, anxiety and desire for vengeance diminish and, sometimes, even disappear completely.

I can even go so far as to say that if belief in the Hereafter had not come to the aid of myself and some of my brothers in the fearsome calamity that is this wrongful imprisonment, we would not have been able to bear a single day of incarceration: it would have been as unbearable as death and might even have driven us to say goodbye to life altogether. But boundless thanks be to God, for despite suffering the distress of my brothers, whom I love as much as my own life; despite the loss and the weeping over thousands of copies of the *Risale-i Nur* and my precious, gilded books, which I love as much as my eyes; and despite the fact I could not bear the slightest insult or stand to be dominated by others, I swear that the light and strength of belief in the Hereafter gave me the patience, endurance, solace, and steadfastness to cope. Indeed, this has given me enthusiasm to gain a greater reward through bearing the painful exertions of my ordeal, for as I said at the outset of this treatise, I considered myself to be a student in a place of instruction worthy of being called the School of Joseph. Were it not for the occasional pains and illnesses of old age, I would have learned my lessons more diligently and with greater ease of mind. However, we have digressed, and for this I hope I will be forgiven.

Also, everyone's home is a small world for them, perhaps even a small paradise. If belief in the Hereafter does not underpin the happiness of that home, the members of that family will suffer anguish and anxiety in proportion to the compassion, love, and attachment they feel for their family. Their paradise will turn into Hell and they will have no option but to numb their minds with temporary amusements and distractions. Like an ostrich that sticks its heads into the sand thinking they cannot be seen by the hunter, these poor people plunge their heads into heedlessness in the hope that death, decline, and separation may not find them. They seek a way out of their terrifying predicament by temporarily anesthetizing themselves. The mother, for example, trembles constantly at seeing her children, for whom she would sacrifice her soul, exposed to danger. Children, for their part, feel constant sorrow and fear at being unable to save their father or siblings from calamities that visit families only too often. Thus, in this tumultuous worldly life, the supposedly contented life of the family loses its happiness in many respects, and the kinship and close connections forged in this brief earthly existence do not result in true loyalty, heartfelt sincerity, disinterested service, or real love. Good character declines proportionately and is often lost completely. However, if belief in the Hereafter enters that home, it illuminates it completely: its members develop respect, love, and compassion for each other, not merely for the sake of relationships in this brief worldly life, but for the sake of their continuance in the eternal realm of happiness that is the Hereafter. They respect, love, and show compassion to each other sincerely; they are loyal to one another and ignore each other's faults and their good character increases accordingly. As a result, the happiness of true humanity begins to develop in the home. Since this too is elucidated in the *Risale-i Nur*, we cut the discussion short here.

Also, a town is like a large home for those who live there. If the members of that large family do not have belief in the Hereafter, rather than sincerity, cordiality, virtue, mutual love and assistance, self-sacrifice, and the seeking of Divine pleasure and otherworldly reward—all of which form the basis of good conduct—vices such as self-interest, pretentiousness, hypocrisy, artificiality, bribery, and deception will dominate. Anarchy and savagery will hold sway beneath the façade of superficial order and a nominal humanity, poisoning the life of the town. The children will become idle troublemakers, the youth will plunge themselves into drunkenness, the powerful will embark on oppression, and the elderly will be left to weep.

By analogy, a country is also a home—the home of a national family. If belief in the Hereafter rules in such a home, sincere respect, earnest compassion, selfless love, mutual assistance, honest service, good social relations, unostentatious charity, and many other excellences and virtues will begin to flourish.

Belief in the Hereafter says to the children: "Stop messing around, for there is Paradise to be won!" and teaches them self-control through instruction from the Qur'an.

It says to the youth: "Hell truly exists: give up your heedlessness!" thus bringing them to their senses.

It says to the oppressor: "Severe torment will be your lot if you continue on this path!" and makes them bow to justice.

It says to the elderly: "In the world to come there exists not only perpetual happiness far greater than anything you could experience in this world, but also eternal youth. Try to win them for yourselves!" thus turning their tears into smiles.

Belief in the Hereafter shows its favorable effects in every group, particular or universal, and illuminates them. Let the sociologists and moral philosophers, who are concerned with the social life of humankind, take note of this. If the rest of the thousands of benefits to be had from belief in the Hereafter are compared with the five or six we have indicated briefly, we can understand that it is only belief that is the means of happiness in this world and the next.

The Fifteenth Ray

Asking the Creator about the Creator Himself

In the Name of God, the All-Merciful, the All-Compassionate.

And from Him do we seek help.

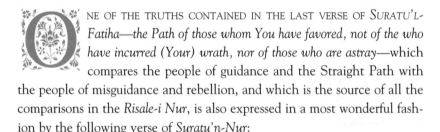NE OF THE TRUTHS CONTAINED IN THE LAST VERSE OF SURATU'L-Fatiha—*the Path of those whom You have favored, not of the who have incurred (Your) wrath, nor of those who are astray*—which compares the people of guidance and the Straight Path with the people of misguidance and rebellion, and which is the source of all the comparisons in the *Risale-i Nur*, is also expressed in a most wonderful fashion by the following verse of *Suratu'n-Nur*:

> God is the Light of the heavens and the earth. The example of His Light is like a niche wherein is a lamp; the lamp is in a crystal, and the crystal is shining as if a pearl-like radiant star, lit from the oil of a blessed olive tree that is neither of the east nor of the west. The oil would almost give light of itself though no fire touches it. Light upon light! God guides to His Light whom He wills. God strikes parables for people. God has full knowledge of all things. (24:35)

and by the verse:

> Or their deeds are like veils of darkness covering up an abysmal sea down into its depths, covered up by a billow, above which is a billow, above which is a cloud: veils of darkness piled one upon another, so that when he stretches out his hand, he can hardly see it. For whomever God has appointed no light, no light has he. (24:40)

The first verse was the main reason for the name "*Nur*" (light) being given to the *Risale-i Nur* (The Treatises of Light). The traveler in The Supreme Sign (*Ayatu'l-Kubra*) questioned the entire universe and all beings in order to seek, find and learn about their Creator. They came to know Him through thirty-three ways and decisive proofs to the degrees of certainty based on knowledge and certainty based on vision or observation. This untiring, insatiable traveler also journeyed through the centuries and the various levels of the heavens and earth with their mind, heart and imagination, inspecting the entire world as though it were a single city. Having their reason dwell now on the Qur'an and now on philosophy, and gazing at the most distant levels through the powerful telescope of imagination, the traveler saw truths as they are in reality and in part informed us of them in The Supreme Sign.

Now, of these many worlds and levels that the traveler entered on their journey of the imagination, which was representational in nature and completely in conformity with reality, only three are explained here in brief in order to illustrate just one aspect of the comparison at the end of *Suratu'l-Fatiha*. It concerns the power of reason. The other visions of the traveler and other comparisons may be found in the relevant parts of *Risale-i Nur*.

THE FIRST EXAMPLE IS SIMILAR TO THE FOLLOWING

The traveler, who has come into the world only to find their Creator and attain knowledge of Him, addresses their reason thus: "We have asked everything about our Creator and have received perfectly satisfying answers. Now, as expressed in the proverb: "In order to learn about the sun one has to ask the sun itself," we will make a further journey in order to gain knowledge of our Creator through the manifestations of His sacred Attributes, such as Knowledge, Will and Power, and through His visible works and the manifestations of His Names." And so the traveler enters the world. Then in the manner of the people of misguidance—those who represent the second current or way mentioned at the end of *Suratu'l-Fatiha*—they embark on the ship of the earth. They put on the spectacles of the science and philosophy that do not follow the wisdom of the Qur'an, and look in accordance with the program of the geography that does not map out the Qur'an. They see the following:

The earth is traveling in an infinite void seventy times faster than a cannon-ball, covering a twenty-thousand-year distance in one year. It has taken upon itself millions of species of wretched, helpless living beings. The traveler realizes that if the earth were to confuse its way for even a minute, or were to collide with a stray star, it would break up and scatter throughout space, pouring all these wretched creatures into nothingness and non-existence. Perceiving the awesome calamity of the current indicated in the verse, *Not of those who have incurred Your wrath, nor of those who are astray,* and the suffocating gloom of the *veils of darkness covering up an abysmal sea down into its depths,* the traveler exclaims: "Alas! What have we done? Why did we get on this terrible ship? How are we to be saved?" Then smashing the spectacles of blind philosophy, the traveler joins the current of *Those whom You have favored (with true guidance).* Suddenly the wisdom of the Qur'an comes to their aid, giving their reason a telescope that shows the exact truth of everything. "Look now!" it says. The traveler looks and sees the following:

The Name "the Lord of the heavens and earth" rises like a sun in the sign of *He it is Who has made the earth subservient to you (like a docile animal), so go about through its shoulders and eat of His provision (67:15).*[28] The Lord has made the earth like a well-organized and secure ship, filling it with living beings together with their provision, and causing it to journey around the sun in the ocean of the universe to attain numerous benefits and instances of wisdom, bringing the produce of the seasons to those who are in need of provision. The Lord has appointed the two angels *Thawr* (Ox) and *Hut* (Fish) as captains of the ship; they steer it on its voyage for the enjoyment of the All-Majestic Creator's creatures and guests, through the magnificent domain of the Lord. The traveler understands that this indicates the truth of *God is the Light of the heavens and the earth,* and thus makes known their Creator through the manifestations of this Name that is the Light. With all their heart and spirit the traveler exclaims: "*All praise and gratitude are for God, the Lord of the worlds,*" and joins the group of *Those whom You have favored.*

The Second example

The second example of what the traveler sees on their journey through the world is as follows:

Leaving the ship of the earth, the traveler enters the world of animals and humankind. They look at that world through the spectacles of the natural science that is devoid of spirit, and sees the following:

---

[28] This verse is miraculous in meaning. It likens the earth to an animal which has been subservient to humankind for its benefits, although it travels very speedily in space. Its *shoulders* are its uplands or mountains, where provision for human beings are found deposited. (Tr.)

These innumerable living creatures have endless needs and are under constant attack from countless harmful enemies and pitiless events, while having a capital with which they can only meet a thousandth, nay, a hundred thousandth of their need. Their power too is perhaps a millionth of what is required to combat these harmful things. Feeling a connection with them on account of being an intelligent being and out of compassion for their fellow beings, the traveler pities them in their terrible plight and feels so sorry for them that they suffer hellish pain. They begin to regret a thousand times over ever having come to this wretched world when suddenly a flash of Qur'anic wisdom comes to their aid, giving them the telescope of *Those whom You have favored*, and saying: "Look!" The traveler looks through it and sees that through the manifestation of *God is the Light of the heavens and the earth*, numerous Divine Names, such as the All-Merciful, the All-Compassionate, the All-Providing, the All-Bestowing, the All-Munificent, and the All-Preserving are each rising like the sun in the signs of verses like: *No living creature is there but He holds it by its forelock* (11:56); *How many a living creature there is that does not carry its own provision in store but God provides for them, and indeed for you* (29:60); *Assuredly We have honored the children of Adam (with many distinctions)* (29:70), and *The virtuous and godly ones will indeed be in (the Gardens of) perpetual bliss* (82:13). Filling the world of humankind and animals with mercy and bounties, they transform it into some sort of temporary Paradise. The traveler now understands that these verses ensure that the All-Munificent Host of this spectacular, instructive guest-house is perfectly known. The traveler repeats a thousand times, *All praise and gratitude are for God, the Lord of the worlds!*

THE THIRD EXAMPLE

What follows is the third example of the hundreds of observations of the traveler during their journey:

The traveler who wants to know their Creator through the manifestations of His Names and Attributes then says to their mind and imagination: "Come! Leaving our bodies behind on the earth, we will ascend to the heavens like the spirits and angels. We will ask the inhabitants of the heavens about our Creator." Their spirit mounts their imagination, their mind mounts their thought, and together they ascended to the heavens. They take astronomy as their guide and look with the view of the philosophy that does not heed the Religion, and the current of *Those who have incurred Your wrath* and *Those who are astray*. The traveler sees the following:

Thousands of heavenly bodies and fiery stars, each a thousand times larger than the earth and moving a hundred times faster than a cannon-ball, are spinning around unconsciously, lifelessly, aimlessly. If one of these bodies happens to lose its way for even a second, it will collide with another unconscious body in that infinite space, causing utter confusion and chaos, like Doomsday.

In whichever direction they look, the traveler is filled with terror and dismay: they are sorry a thousand times over that they have ascended to the heavens. Their mind and imagination are extremely upset and bewildered. The mind and imagination exclaim: "Our duty is to see and point out fine truths. We no longer want to observe or know such infernally ugly and tormenting spectacles; we withdraw from this task!" Then suddenly, through the manifestation of *God is the Light of the heavens and the earth*, numerous Names such as "the Creator of the heavens and the earth", "the Subjugator of the sun and moon", and "the Lord of the worlds" each rise like a sun in the signs of verses such as *And We have adorned the lowest heaven (the heaven of the world) with lamps* (67:5); *Do they, then, never observe the sky above them, how We have constructed it and adorned it?* (50:6), and ... *then He directed (His Knowledge, Will, Power, and Favor) to the heaven, and formed it into seven heavens* (2:20). They fill all the heavens with light and with angels, transforming it into a huge mosque and military encampment. The traveler enters the current of *Those whom You have favored*, and is saved from that of *Those who are astray* and *veils of darkness covering up an abysmal sea down into its depths*. The traveler sees a well-organized, beautiful, and magnificent land, as wonderful as Paradise itself. Observing that its inhabitants are making known the All-Majestic Creator, the value of the traveler's mind and imagination increases a thousand times over, and so does their task.

Referring to the *Risale-i Nur* the other observations of the traveler, which are comparable with these three, and the knowledge of the Necessarily Existent One which is acquired through the manifestations of His Names, here we will mention only certain brief indications. Like that traveler through the world, we will try to become acquainted very briefly with the Creator of the universe through the works and manifestations of Knowledge, Will, and Power, which are three of His seven sacred Attributes. For a detailed explanation, we refer you to the relevant parts of *the Risale-i Nur*.

The Twenty-ninth Gleam

Why belief is the greatest blessing for humankind

This chapter concerns the phrase *All praise and gratitude are for God.*

In this short treatise, out of endless benefits and lights of belief which lead people to declare *All praise and gratitude are for God*, only eight will be expounded.

In the Name of God, the All-Merciful, the All-Compassionate.

First point

FIRST OF ALL, THE FOLLOWING TWO THINGS SHOULD BE POINTED OUT:

- Philosophy (which does not obey the Religion) is a pair of dark glasses which shows everything to be ugly and frightful. On the contrary, true religious belief is a transparent, clear, radiant pair of spectacles which shows everything to be beautiful and lovable.
- Because they are connected with all creatures, having a sort of transaction with all things, and are by nature compelled to meet, converse and be neighborly with the things that surround them, humans have six sides or aspects: left, right, front, back, above and below.

On wearing either of the two pairs of spectacles mentioned, humans can see the creatures and circumstances that are on these sides.

THE RIGHT SIDE: What is meant by this side or aspect is the past. When the past is viewed through the spectacles of irreligious philosophy, it appears to be a vast, dark, terrifying, overturned graveyard, whose doomsday already seems to have come to pass. It is doubtless that this sight causes humans great terror, fear and despair.

However, when this side is seen through the spectacles of belief, even if this realm appears to have been overturned, there has been no loss of life. Instead one understands that its crew and inhabitants have been transferred to a better, light-filled world. The graves and pits are considered to be underground tunnels, dug to lead to another, light-filled world. This means that the rejoice, relief, contentment and peace of mind which belief affords humans is a Divine favor which makes them utter thousands of times over: "All praise and gratitude are for God!"

THE LEFT SIDE: The left side represents the future. Now when the future is viewed through the spectacles of philosophy, it appears in the form of a vast, dark, frightening grave which is going to rot us and make us food for snakes and scorpions. But when viewed through the spectacles of belief, it appears in the form of a banquet prepared for humans by God Almighty, the Creator, the All-Merciful and the All-Compassionate, complete with all manner of the finest and most delicious foods and drinks. And it makes them utter thousands of times: "All praise and gratitude are for God!"

ABOVE: When someone uses the spectacles of philosophy to look upwards toward the heavens, they feel an awful dread and terror at the extremely rapid and varied movements of the billions of stars and heavenly bodies, racing like wild horses around in endless space. However, when a believer looks at them, they see that just as army maneuvers are carried out under the supervision and on the orders of a commander, the stars are light-diffusing lamps that adorn the world of the heavens. Consequently, rather than feeling terror and dread at those horses racing, they are filled with friendliness and love. It is surely little to say "All praise and gratitude are for God!" thousands of times in return for the bounty of belief, which depicts the world of the heavens in such a benign way.

BELOW: When someone uses the eye of philosophy to gaze at the earth below his feet, he sees that it resembles an animal left unbridled to wander aimlessly around the sun, or a scuppered boat without a captain, and they are struck with terror and anxiety. But when they look through the prism of belief, they see it as a ship of the All-Merciful, taking humankind on a pleasure cruise around the sun under the command of God Almighty, with all necessary food, drink and clothing on board. And so they begin to utter "All praise and gratitude are for God!" wholeheartedly for this great bounty which issues from belief.

THE FRONT: If a person who indulges in philosophy looks at this side, they see that all living creatures, whether humans or beasts, are disappearing convoy by convoy and with great speed. That is to say, they are going to non-existence and ceasing to be. Since they know that they too are condemned to the same end, they almost lose their mind with grief. But for a believer who views the same thing with the eye of belief, the people traveling on this side are not going to the world of non-existence; rather, they are being transferred from one pasture to another, like nomads. They are migrating from a transitory realm to an eternally permanent one; from the farm on which they have labored to the office where they collect their wages; from a place of hardship and difficulty to one of ease and mercy. And so they view this aspect with pleasure and gratitude.

Apparent difficulties which emerge along the road, such as death and the grave, are in fact means of happiness with respect to their results. For the road which leads to the light-filled worlds passes through the grave, and the greatest happiness comes as the result of the worst, most grievous disasters. For example, Prophet Joseph, upon him be peace, attained the happiness of being vice-ruler of Egypt only after he had been thrown into a well by his brothers and put in prison on account of the slander of Zulaikha.[29] Likewise, a child coming into the world from its mother's womb attains happiness in this world only as a result of the tiresome, crushing difficulties he or she suffers along the way.

THE BACK: When one looks through the prism of philosophy at those who come from behind, they can find no answer to the question: "Where have they come from and where are they going? And why did they come to the realm of this world?" Naturally the questioner remains in a torment of bewilderment and doubt. But if they look through the prism of belief, they will understand that human beings are observers that are sent to the world by the Eternal Sovereign to contemplate and study the amazing miracles of Power displayed in the exhibition of the universe. After having received their grades in accordance with the level at which they grasp the value and grandeur of those miracles of the Power and the extent to which they point to the Grandeur of the Eternal Sovereign, human beings will return to the realm of the Eternal Sovereign. And so they will say, "All praise and gratitude are for God!" for the favor of belief which has led them to this blessing of understanding.

---

[29] According to certain Muslim historians, Zulaykha is the name of the wife of the minister, who bought the Prophet Joseph, upon him be peace, as a slave. She sought to enjoy herself by him, but when the Prophet Joseph rejected her, she ordered him to be imprisoned. See the Qur'an, 12:23–35. (Tr.)

Since the praise offered in saying, "All praise and gratitude are for God!" for the favor of belief, which thus removes the above-mentioned layers of darkness, is also a blessing or favor, it also requires praise and thanks. This in turn requires the offering of praise and thanks a third time, which in turn requires them a fourth time, and so on, forming an infinite chain of praise that is born of a single uttering of the phrase: "All praise and gratitude are for God!"

Second point

We should say, "All praise and gratitude are for God!" for the bounty of belief which illuminates these six sides, for in addition to being a great favor or blessing on account of dispelling the darkness of the six sides and therefore warding off evil, belief is also a bounty and a favor in respect of the fact that it illuminates these sides and thus attracts benefits. Therefore since humans are by nature civilized, they are connected with all the creatures on the six sides, and have the possibility of benefiting from these sides through the favor of belief.

Thus according to a meaning of the verse, *To whatever direction you turn, there is the "Face" of God* (2:115), humans find enlightenment on whichever of the six sides they are. In fact, a believer has a life which in effect extends from the foundation of the world to its end. This life of theirs benefits from the light of a life which extends from pre-eternity to post-eternity. Also, thanks to belief, which illuminates the six sides, the present narrow time and space in which humans find themselves are transformed into a spacious world. This extensive world becomes like their house, while the past and the future become like present time for their spirit and heart: the distance between them disappears.

Third point

Since belief provides points of support and assistance, it requires the response "All praise and gratitude are for God!"

Humanity needs a source of support or reliance because of their impotence and the multiplicity of their adversaries, so that they may seek refuge in that source to repel those who are ranged against them. Likewise, because of the abundance of their needs and their extreme innate poverty, they are in need of a source of assistance from which they may seek help, so that through it they may meet their needs.

O humankind! Your one and only point of support or reliance is belief in God. The only source of assistance for your spirit and conscience is belief in the Hereafter. Therefore, one who is unaware of these two sources suffers constant fear in their heart and spirit, and their conscience is continually tormented. However, the person who relies on the first point and asks for help from the second experiences numerous pleasures and instances of friendliness in their heart and spirit: as a result they become consoled and their conscience finds rest and satisfaction.

Fourth point

The light of belief removes the pain which arises from the imminent vanishing of lawful pleasures by showing that similar pleasures always exist and will come again in the future. Furthermore, by indicating the source of bounties, it ensures that those bounties continue eternally and do not diminish.

Also, by showing the pleasure of the union with pleasures similar to them, it removes the pain of separation and parting. That is to say, a single pleasure contains many pains due to the thought of separation, while belief removes them by calling to mind the recurrence of that pleasure. There are further pleasures in the renewal of pleasure. If the tree from which a fruit is taken is unknown, the pleasure restricted to the fruit disappears when it is eaten up, which causes sorrow. But if the tree is known, there is no pain when the fruit ceases to exist, for there are other fruits which can be picked from that tree to take its place.

In fact, renewal itself is a pleasure. For what causes the human spirit the greatest distress are the pains that arise from separation. The light of belief removes the pains of separation from pleasures through their replacement by similar ones, and through the hope of attaining them.

Fifth point

The light of belief shows the things that humans imagine to be strange and hostile to them, or to be lifeless and lost as though orphans among creatures, as friends and siblings, as living, and as glorifiers of God. That is to say, a person who looks with the eye of heedlessness supposes the beings in the world to be harmful like enemies, and they take fright: they see everything as alien. For in the view of misguidance, there are no bonds of brotherhood between the things of the past and those of the future: there is only an insignificant, partial relationship between them. Consequently, the brotherhood of the people of misguidance is only like a minute out of thousands of years.

In the view of belief, all bodies are living, familiar and friendly with one another. Belief also shows each of them to be glorifying its Creator through the tongue of its being. It is in this respect that all bodies have a sort of life and spirit appropriate to each. Therefore there is nothing fearful or frightening about bodies when they are viewed in the light of belief; instead there is friendliness and love.

The view of misguidance considers human beings, powerless as they are to secure their demands and aspirations, as ownerless and without protector; it sees them grieving and sorrowful, like weeping orphans because of their impotence. By contrast, the view of belief sees living creatures not as orphans but as officials charged with certain tasks, as servants charged with the duty of glorifying and extolling God.

Sixth point

The light of belief depicts this world and the Hereafter as two tables filled with numerous varieties of bounties: believers benefit by accessing them with the hand of belief, with their inner and external senses, and their spiritual faculties. Seen through the prism of misguidance, the sphere of benefit for living beings diminishes and is restricted to material pleasures. Seen through the prism of belief, however, it expands to a sphere which encompasses the heavens and the earth. Truly, believers consider the sun to be a lamp hanging in the roof of their house, and the moon to be a night-light. For this reason, the sun and the moon are bounties and examples of Divine grace for them, and the sphere from which believers benefit is broader than the heavens. Through the eloquence of its verses, *He has made the sun and the moon constant in their courses, and so serviceable to you* (14:33), and *He has made all that is in the heavens and all that is on the earth of service to you* (31:20), the miraculously eloquent Qur'an points to these wonderful favors and blessings which arise from belief.

Seventh point

It is known through belief that God's Existence is a great favor that surpasses all others; it is a source, a fountain, which contains endless varieties of favors, innumerable sorts of blessings and uncountable kinds of gifts. It is therefore incumbent upon humans to repay this debt by offering praise and laudation for the favors of belief to the number of particles in creation. Some of these favors have been pointed out in various parts of the *Risale-i Nur* where belief in God is discussed.

One of the favors for which praise and thanks should be offered by saying *al-hamdu li'llah* ("All praise and gratitude are for God!")—by mentioning the word *hamd* (praise) with the definite article *al*, in the form of *al-hamdu*, meaning "all praise"—is the favor of God's being the All-Merciful. God's Mercifulness refers to, and is the source of, favors and bounties as numerous as the living beings which need and are favored with mercy. For a human being in particular is connected with all living creatures, and because of this, he or she becomes happy on account of their happiness and is saddened by their pains. Thus a favor enjoyed by a single individual is a favor also for their fellows.

God has another important Attribute, namely Compassion. His being the All-Compassionate comprises, and is the source of, bounties as numerous as the children and young favored with their mothers' tenderness, and therefore deserves praise and laudation accordingly. A person with conscience who feels sorrow and pity at the weeping of a motherless, hungry child, surely feels pleasure on seeing a mother's compassion for her children: they are pleased and happy with it. Thus pleasures of this sort are all favors and require praise and thanks.

Another of the bounties or favors which requires praise and thanks to the number of all the varieties and instances of wisdom contained in the universe is Divine Wisdom or God's being the All-Wise. For just as a person's soul is favored with the manifestations of Divine Mercy and their heart with the manifestations of Divine Compassion, their intellect also derives pleasure from the subtleties of Divine Wisdom. Therefore they require endless praise and laudation through the loud utterance of "All praise and gratitude are for God!"

Also, Divine Preservation or God's being the All-Preserving is another favor for which praise should be offered with an "All praise and gratitude are for God!" so great that it would fill all space with its sound—it should be offered as many times as there are manifestations of the Divine Name the All-Inheriting, as there are descendants who continue to live after the death of their forebears, as there are beings in the next world, and as there are actions of humans which are preserved so that they may receive their rewards in the Hereafter. For the continuation of a favor is more valuable than the favor itself; the permanence of pleasure is more pleasurable than the pleasure itself; eternal permanence in Paradise is superior to Paradise itself, and so on. Consequently, with all the bounties it contains, Almighty God's Attribute of Preservation is far greater than, and far superior to, all the bounties which exist throughout the universe. Thus this Attribute requires an "All praise and gratitude are for God!" so great that it would fill the world. You can compare the rest of the Divine Names and Attributes with the four mentioned here, and since in each there are endless bounties or favors, each requires endless praise and thanks.

Likewise, Prophet Muhammad, upon him be peace and blessings, who is the means of attaining the favor of belief, which has the authority to open all the treasuries of bounties, is also such a favor that humankind owes him the debt of extolling and applauding him throughout eternity.

Similarly, the favors of Islam and the Qur'an, which are the concentrated form and source of all varieties of bounties, both material and spiritual, require and deserve infinite praise.

Eighth point

All praise and gratitude be to God that, as established by the mighty Qur'an with all its chapters and sections, all its pages and lines, and all its words and letters, this cosmic book known as the universe praises and extols Him, the All-Pure and Holy One, through making manifest His Attributes of Beauty and Grace and Perfection. It is as follows:

According to its capacity, however great or small, each embroidery of this cosmic book praises and extols its Embroiderer, Who is the One and Eternally Besought, through manifesting His Attributes of Majesty. Also, through displaying His Attributes of Beauty and Grace, each inscription in this book extols its Inscriber, Who is the All-Merciful and the All-Compassionate. Besides, on account of being favored with and mirroring the manifestations of the Divine All-Beautiful Names, all the inscriptions, points and embroideries of this book praise and extol the All-Pure and Holy One through lauding, glorifying and exalting Him. Furthermore, each ode in this book extols and glorifies its Composer, Who is the All-Powerful and the All-Knowing.

Gleams of Truth

Flowers from the seeds of truth

In the Name of God, the All-Merciful, the All-Compassionate.

In an assembly in the World of Representations or Ideal Forms

Comparisons between Islam and modern civilization,
and between scientific genius and the guidance of Islam

IN A TRUE DREAM ON A FRIDAY NIGHT AT THE BEGINNING OF THE period of truce following World War I, I was asked by a supreme assembly in the World of Representations and Ideal Forms:

"What will emerge in the Muslim world following the defeat?" I replied, as the representative of the present age, and they listened to me:

From the times of its foundation, this State saw itself as duty-bound to sacrifice itself for the Islamic world and as the standard-bearer of the Caliphate,

And accordingly it undertook *jihad*, a collective religious obligation, to maintain Islamic independence and exalt the Word of God.

Over time, the calamity that has struck this State, this Muslim nation, will certainly bring prosperity and freedom to the Muslim world.

This present disaster will be compensated for in the future. One who loses three and gains three hundred in return makes no loss. As a zealous laborer, they change their present for a better future.

For this calamity has aroused compassion and Islamic solidarity and brotherhood, the yeast or catalyst of our lives, to an extraordinary degree; it has given a wonderful impetus to our brotherhood.

The present civilization will change form, and its corrupt system will be demolished; it is then that an Islamic civilization will emerge. Muslims will certainly be the first to enter it voluntarily.

If you want a comparison between the civilization of the Shari'a and the present one, closely examine the principles of each and consider their consequences:

The principles of present-day civilization are negative. Its foundations and values are five negative principles. Its machinery is based on these.

Its point of support and reliance is might or force rather than right, and the basic characteristic of force is aggression and hostility, from which treachery arises.

Its goal is, instead of virtue, the gratification of mean self-interest, the essential characteristic of which is conflict and rivalry, and the consequence of which is crime.

Its law of life is conflict rather than cooperation and mutual helping; the essential characteristic of conflict is contention and mutual repulsion; the consequence is poverty.

Its basic bond between peoples is racism or racial discrimination, which develops to the detriment of others; it is nourished and strengthened by the right of others being devoured.

Negative nationalism or racism paves the way for constant, terrible clashes, disastrous collisions; the result is destruction.

The fifth is this: the enchanting service of the present civilization excites lusts and passions, facilitating the gratification of animal desires; the consequence is dissipation.

The basic characteristic of lusts and passions is always this: they transform humans into beasts, changing their character; they deform them, perverting their humanity.

Most of these civilized people—if you were to turn them inside out—would appear as apes and foxes, snakes, bears, and swine. Their characters have appointed their forms. They appear to the imagination in their furs and skins!

By contrast, the Shari'a is the balance of the earth. The mercy in the Shari'a comes from the heaven of the Qur'an. The principles of the Qur'anic civilization are positive. Its mechanism for happiness turns on five positive principles:

Its point of support and reliance is right instead of might and the unchanging characteristic of right is justice and balance, which give rise to salvation, security and well-being, removing wretchedness and villainy.

Its aim is virtue instead of self-interest and the basic character of virtue is love and mutual attraction. Happiness arises from these, and enmity disappears.

Its principle in life is cooperation instead of conflict and killing, and the essential characteristic of cooperation is unity and solidarity; these enliven the community.

In place of lust and passion, its form of service is guidance and the essential characteristic of guidance is progress and prosperity in a way that is befitting to humanity, as well as enlightenment and perfection in a way that is required by the spirit.

While racism and negative nationalism destroy the point of unity among the masses, the bonds the Shari'a establishes between peoples are those of religion, citizenship, profession, and the brotherhood of belief.

The basic characteristics of these bonds are sincere brother/sisterhood, and general salvation, security and well-being. The Shari'a only demands self-defense in the case of external attacks.

Now you have understood why Muslims have remained distant from the present civilization without adopting it.

Up to the present, Muslims have not entered this present civilization voluntarily, it has not suited them; rather, on them have been clamped the fetters of bondage.

While it should have been the cure for humankind, this civilization has become the poison. It has cast eighty per cent of the population into destitution and misery and given false happiness to ten per cent.

The remaining ten per cent has been left uneasy, stranded between the two. The profits that come from trade have gone to the tyrannical minority. But true happiness is the happiness shared by all, or at least salvation for the majority.

The Qur'an, revealed as a mercy for humankind, only accepts civilization of the kind that brings happiness to all, or at least to the majority. In the present civilization, passions are unrestricted, impulses and fancies too are free; this is an animal freedom.

Passions dominate people, impulses and fancies too are despotic; they have made unnecessary needs essential ones, and banished ease and relief.

While in primitive life a person was in need of four things, civilization has made them needy of a hundred, and impoverished them.

Lawful labor is insufficient to meet the cost. This has driven humanity towards fraud and the unlawful. It is due to this that civilization has corrupted the essence of morality.

It has given certain wealth and glitter to society and the human species, but it has made the individual immoral and indigent. There are numerous testimonies to this.

All of the savagery and crimes in former times and all the cruelty and treachery have been vomited by this malignant civilization all at once, and its stomach is still retching.[30]

The fact that the Islamic world is able to remain aloof is both meaningful and noteworthy. It has been reluctant to accept this civilization, and has acted coldly.

Truly, the distinguishing quality of the Divine light in the illustrious Shari'a is independence and self-sufficiency.

It is due to this quality that the light of guidance has never allowed the genius of Rome, the spirit of (European) civilization, to dominate it.

The guidance of the Shari'a cannot be combined with the philosophy of the latter, nor be grafted onto it, nor follow it.

The compassion and the dignity of belief to be found in the spirit of Islam, and the truths of the Shari'a which it has nourished—the Qur'an of miraculous exposition has taken the truths of the Shari'a in its shining hand;

Each of these truths of the Shari'a is a Staff of Moses in that shining hand. In the future that sorcerer civilization will prostrate in wonderment before it.

Now, note this: there were two geniuses—Ancient Greece and Rome, those twins from a single stock. One was imaginative, the other materialist.

Like water and oil, they never combined. Such a phenomenon required time, civilization strove to do so and Christianity tried, but none has been able to combine them.

---

[30] That is, the civilization will vomit more terribly. It has vomited in the form of the two world wars in such a fashion that it has soiled the air, ground, and sea, staining them with blood.

Both preserved their partial independence. They have remained as if two spirits (in a single body); now they have changed their bodies; one has become German, the other French.

They have experienced a sort of reincarnation. O my dream-brother! This is what time has shown. Those twin geniuses have rejected any moves to combine them;

They are still not reconciled. Since they are twins, they are brothers and friends, companions in progress; but they have fought and never made peace.

How could it therefore be that the light of the Qur'an and the guidance of the Shari'a, when it has a completely different source, origin, and place of appearance, is reconciled with the genius of Rome, the spirit of modern civilization, and should join and combine with it?

That genius and this guidance – their origins are different: guidance descends from the heavens, genius emerges from the earth. Guidance works in the heart and genius works in the mind.

Genius works in the mind and confuses the heart. Guidance illuminates the spirit, making its seeds sprout and flourish; dark human nature is illuminated by it.

The capacity of guidance for perfection suddenly advances; it makes the carnal soul a docile servant; it gives zealous and endeavoring humans an angelic countenance.

As for genius, it focuses its attention primarily on the carnal soul and physical being; it comes into nature, making the soul an arable field and the carnal potentials develop and flourish;

It subjugates the spirit, causing the seeds to dry up; it displays satanic features in humankind. But guidance gives happiness to both lives—this and the next—and spreads light in both this world and the next, elevating humankind.

Genius, like Antichrist blind in one eye, sees only this life and this world; it is materialist and world-adoring. It turns humans into beasts.

Genius worships deaf nature and serves blind force. But guidance recognizes the conscious Art (manifested as nature) and turns to the wise Power (that gives existence to nature). Genius draws a veil of ingratitude over the earth while guidance scatters the light of thanks.

It is because of this that genius is deaf and blind, while guidance is hearing and seeing. In the view of genius, the bounties of the earth are ownerless booty;

It prompts the desire to usurp and steal them thanklessly, to savagely snap them off from nature.

In the view of guidance, the bounties scattered over the breast of the earth and the face of the universe are the fruits of Mercy; it sees a gracious hand beneath every bounty, and has kissed it in gratitude.

I cannot deny that there are numerous virtues in civilization, but they are neither the property of Christianity, nor the invention of Europe.

Nor are they the product of this century; they are the common property of humanity, produced as the result of the conjunction of thoughts and studies over time, from the laws of the revealed religions, and emerge out of innate need,

And particularly from the Islamic revolution brought about by the Shari'a of Muhammad. No one can claim ownership of these.

The leader of the assembly from the World of Representations asked another question:

QUESTION: "Calamities are always the result of treachery but pave the way for reward. O man of the present century! Divine Destiny has dealt a blow and Divine Decree has passed sentence.

"What did you do so that both the Divine Decree and Destiny have so judged you—that the Divine Decree has sentenced you to this calamity and given you a beating?

"It is always the error of the majority which causes general disasters."

I said in reply:

ANSWER: Humankind's misguided thinking, Nimrod-like obstinacy, Pharaoh-like haughtiness grew and grew on the earth until they reached the heavens. Humanity also offended the sensitive mystery of creation.

It caused the shudders of the last war to pour down from the heavens like the plague and deluge; it caused a heavenly blow to be dealt to the infidel.

This means, the calamity was the calamity of all humankind. The common cause, inclusive of all humankind, was the misguided thinking that arose from materialism – bestial freedom, the despotism of carnal desires and fancies.

Our share in it resulted from our neglect and abandonment of the pillars of Islam. For the Creator the All-Exalted wanted one hour out of the twenty-four.

He ordered us, willed that we, for our good, assign one hour for the five daily Prayers. But out of laziness we gave them up, neglected them in heedlessness.

So we received the following punishment: He made us perform Prayers of a sort during these last five years through a constant, twenty-four hour drill and hardship, keeping us ceaselessly moving and striving.

He also demanded of us one month a year for fasting, but we pitied our carnal souls, so in atonement He compelled us to fast for five years.

He wanted us to pay as *Zakah* either a fortieth or a tenth of the property He gave us, but out of miserliness we did wrong: we mixed the unlawful with our property, and did not give the *Zakah* voluntarily.

So He had our accumulated *Zakah* taken from us, and saved us from what was unlawful in our property. The deed causes the punishment of its kind. The punishment is of the same as the deed.[31]

Good, righteous acts are of two sorts: one positive and voluntary, the other negative and enforced. All pains and calamities are good deeds, but they are negative and enforced. The *hadith* that tells us of this[32] offers consolation.

---

[31] I did not mention the *Hajj* in the dream, for neglect of the *Hajj* and its wisdom drew not calamity, but Divine Wrath, and the punishment it incurred was not atonement for our sins but an increase in our sins. It was the neglect of the elevated Islamic policy, which exists in the *Hajj* and brings unity of views through mutual acquaintance and cooperation through mutual assistance, and it was neglect of the vast social benefits contained in the *Hajj* which have prepared the ground for the enemy to employ millions of Muslims against Islam. Those were Indian Muslims! Thinking that he was their enemy, they killed their father (the Ottoman State), and now they are weeping beside his dead body. There are the Tatars and the Caucasian peoples! They understood that the one in whose killing they had collaborated with the enemy was their poor mother, but it was too late! They are weeping at her feet. These are the Arabs! They mistakenly killed their heroic brother, and now in their bewilderment they do not even know how to weep. These are the Africans! They killed their brother unknowingly, now they are lamenting. This is the Muslim world; it heedlessly helped the enemy kill its standard-bearing son, now it is pulling its hair out, groaning and lamenting. Instead of hastening to the *Hajj* eagerly, which is pure good, millions of Muslims have been made to make long journeys under the enemy flag, which is pure evil. Ponder on this and take heed!

[32] The Pride of humankind says: "In whatever circumstance a believer is, it is to his good. This is not so for anyone other than believers. For if something happy happens to him, he thanks

This sinful nation has made its ablutions in blood; it has repented with deeds. As an immediate reward, four million, a fifth of this nation, were raised to the degree of sainthood through the rank of martyrdom or warring for God's sake; this wiped out their sin.

The elevated assembly from the World of Representations appreciated these words.

I woke up suddenly; rather, this was a meeting in true wakefulness before I went to sleep. In my view, wakefulness is a dream and a dream is a sort of wakefulness.

There I was the representative of this age, and here I am Said Nursi!

All true pain is in misguidance, and all true pleasure in belief: a mighty truth dressed in imagination

Sensible fellow-traveler! O beloved friend! If you want to clearly perceive the differences between the luminous way of the *Straight Path* and the dark path of *those who have incurred God's wrath* and *those who are astray,*

Come, take your fancy and mount your imagination, together we will go into the darkness of non-existence. We will visit that vast grave, that city full of the dead.

An Eternal All-Powerful One took us out of the darkness of non-existence with His hand of Power, mounted us on existence, and sent us to this world, this city without pleasures.

Now we have come to the world of existence, this fearful desert. Our eyes have opened and we have looked in the six directions.

Firstly, we look before us seeking mercy and help, but tribulations and pain attack us like enemies. We take fright at this and retreat.

We look to left and right to the natural elements, seeking help. But we see their hearts are hard and merciless. They grind their teeth, looking at us angrily and threateningly. They heed neither plea nor plaint.

Like helpless creatures, we despairingly lift our gazes upwards. Seeking help, we look to the heavenly bodies, but see them to be threatening.

As though each was a bomb; having shot from of their housings they are speeding through space. But somehow they do not touch one another.

God, and this is to his good. If some harm touches him, he remains patient, and this also is to his good." (*Muslim*, "Zuhd" 64; *ad-Darimi*, "Riqaq" 61.) (Tr.)

If one confused its way accidentally, this visible, corporeal world would be blown to pieces; God forbid! They move dependent on chance; no good can come of them.

In despair we turn back our gaze from that direction, overcome by painful bewilderment. We bow our heads, bent over our breasts; we look to ourselves, pondering and studying our own selves.

Now we hear the shouts of myriad needs coming from our wretched selves. The cries of thousands of desires issue forth. While hoping for solace, we take fright.

No good comes from that either. Seeking refuge, we consult our conscience or conscious nature; we look into it seeking a means and seeking help. Alas, again we are left unaided; we have to help our conscious nature.

For in it are thousands of aspirations, seething desires, wild emotions, all extending throughout the universe. We tremble with all of them, and cannot offer help.

Left unaided between existence and non-existence, these aspirations extend to eternity in the past on one side and eternity in the future on the other. They are so extensive. Even if the conscious nature were to swallow the world, it would still not be satisfied.

Whatever we have had recourse to on this painful path, we have encountered calamities. For the paths of *those who have incurred God's wrath* and *those who are astray* are thus. It is chance and misguidance which lead us on these paths.

It is we who have allowed chance and misguidance to lead us, and so we have fallen into our present state. We are in such a state that we have forgotten the beginning of existence and the end of the world, as well as the Maker and the resurrection of the dead.

We are in a state that is worse than Hell; it scorches more terribly and it crushes our spirits. We had recourse to these six directions, but the result was this state.

It is a merciless state, comprising fear and terror, impotence and trembling, alarm and isolation, being orphaned and despair.

Now we will take up fronts opposite each of the directions (from where we had sought mercy and help, only to fall into a merciless state) and try to repulse them. Firstly, we have recourse to our own strength, but alas! We are powerless, weak.

Secondly, we turn to our souls, hoping their needs can be silenced. But alas! We see that they cry out unceasingly.

Thirdly, we cry out for help, seeking a savior; but there is no one to hear and respond. We think everything is hostile, everything strange. Nothing consoles our hearts; nothing gives a sense of security or true pleasure.

Fourthly, the more we look at the celestial bodies, the more they fill us with fear and awe. A feeling of terrifying loneliness, which vexes the conscience, appears; it torments the mind and fills us with delusions.

Brother! That is the path of misguidance! On it we experienced all the darkness of unbelief. Come, now, my brother, we will turn again to non-existence.

Again we will come. This time our way is the Straight Path and the way of belief. Our guide and leader are Divine Grace and the Qur'an, the Falcon that flies over the centuries.

At one time, the Eternal Sovereign's Mercy and Grace willed our existence, His Power brought us forth, graciously mounting us on the law of His Will, completing us stage after stage.

Then It compassionately clothed us in the garment of existence, bestowing on us the rank of undertaking the Supreme Trust,[33] whose decorations are supplication and the obligatory Prayers.

All of these stages are mansions of bestowal on our long road. To make our journey easy, the Divine Destiny has inscribed a decree on the parchment of our foreheads;

Wherever we go, with whichever group we are guests, we are welcomed in truly brotherly fashion. We give of our belongings, and we receive from theirs: a delightful trade.

They nourish us, adorn us with gifts, then see us off on our way. Now at last we have come to the door of the world. We hear a noise.

See, we have arrived on the earth. We have set foot in the visible world. Here is a promenade and festival, organized by the All-Merciful for the clamorous habitation of humankind.

---

[33] The Supreme Trust is the human ego or being human or human nature as the focus of the manifestations of God's Names that are manifested throughout the universe. (Tr.)

We know nothing at all, our guide and leader is the Will of the All-Merciful. Our delicate eyes are the deputy of this guide. We open our eyes and look around. Do we recall the former time from where we came?

We were strangers, orphans, we had many enemies. We did not know who our protector was. Now, with the light of belief, which is a strong pillar, we find in us a point of support and a point of help against those enemies.

Our protector, belief in God, repulses our enemies. It is the light of our spirits, the light of our lives, and the spirit of our spirits. Now our hearts are easy and we disregard the enemies, not even recognizing them as such.

When on our former journey we consulted our conscious nature, we heard innumerable cries, laments, and complaints.

And so we were overcome by calamities. Now, our aspirations and desires, our capacity and senses, constantly desire eternity. But we did not know how to obtain it. We were ignorant of how to obtain it and our conscious nature lamented and cried.

However, all praise and gratitude be to God, this time we have found a point of help; it constantly gives life to our capacity and aspirations, making them take flight for eternity.

It shows them the way, and from that encouraging, mysterious point—belief in God—our capacity receives help, drinks the water of life, and races to its perfection.

The second pole of belief is affirmation of the Resurrection, the resurrection of the dead and eternal happiness. Belief is the pearl of this shell and the Qur'an is its proof. Human conscience is a mystery indicating it.

Now raise your head and take a look at the universe. Speak to it. On our former way how awesome it appeared. Now it is smiling on every side, gracefully winking and speaking.

Do you not see—our eyes have become like bees? They fly everywhere in the garden of the universe, around the multitude of flowers; each flower offers these bees delicious nectar.

Each flower also offers friendliness, solace, and love. Our eyes collect them and bring back the pollen of testimony. They make the most delicious honey flow forth.

As our gaze alights on the movements of the heavenly bodies—the stars, or suns—they give the Creator's wisdom in its hands. Learning important lessons and the manifestation of His Mercy, it takes flight.

It is as though the sun is speaking to us, saying: "My brothers and sisters! Do not feel lonely or frightened. You are welcome, how good of you to have come! This dwelling place is yours; I am but a candle-holder.

"I am like you, naught but a pure, absolutely obedient servant. Out of His utter mercy, the Unique and Eternally Besought One has made me a servant of light for you. Light and heat are from me, supplication and Prayer from you!"

Now look at the moon! And the stars and the seas; each says in its own tongue: "Welcome! It's good of you to have come! Do you not recognize us?"

Look through the mystery of cooperation, lend an ear to the signs of the order. Each says: "We are all servants, mirrors of the All-Majestic One's Mercy; do not worry, do not become weary or fearful of us!

"Let not the roars of the thunder and cries of events rouse in you fear or suspicion, for within them reverberate Divine recitations, glorifications, supplications, and entreaties.

"The All-Majestic One, Who sent you to us, holds their reins in His hands. The eye of belief reveals the signs of Mercy on their faces; each proclaims It."

O believer with a wakeful heart! Let our eyes rest a little; now in their place we will hand over our sensitive ears to the blessed hands of belief. We will send them to the world to listen to its delightful tune.

The voices and sounds that we thought were universal mourning and lamentations of death on our former way are in fact supplications and prayers, cries of glorification.

Listen to the murmuring of the air, the twittering of birds, the pattering of the rain, the splashing of the seas, the crashing of thunder, the crackling of stones; all are meaningful sounds of prayer and glorification.

The melodies of the air, the roars of the thunder, the strains of the waves are all recitations of Divine Grandeur. The chanting of the rain, the chirruping of the birds are all glorifications of Mercy—indications of truth is uttered in their languages.

The sounds of things are all sounds of existence: "I too exist," they say. The silent-seeming universe speaks uninterruptedly: "Do not suppose us to be lifeless, O chattering fellow!"

It is either the pleasure of bounty or the descent of mercy that makes the birds sing. With their different voices, their songs, they applaud mercy, alight on bounties, and take flight with thanks.

Implicitly they say: "Beings of the universe, O brothers and sisters! What fine conditions we live in; we are tenderly nourished, we are happy with our lot!" With beaks pointed to the heavens they send their cheerful songs through the air.

The universe is a lofty orchestra in its entirety; its recitations are heard through the light of belief. For wisdom rejects the existence of chance and the order in existence banishes any formation or event from being attributable to random coincidence.

Fellow-traveler! We are now leaving this world of representations, stepping down from the realm of images. We will stop in the field of reason, follow the ways we have traveled that lie before our eyes and compare them.

Our first, painful way is that of *those who have incurred God's wrath*, and *those who are astray*. It inflicts suffering on the conscience, in its innermost part; suffering and severe pain. Consciousness shows this; we traveled that way in opposition to our conscience.

We must be saved from it, we need to be—either the pain must be alleviated, or human feeling numbed—we cannot endure it otherwise, for our cries for help are not heeded.

Guidance is healing, but carnal tendencies and fancies block out the feelings. Submission to carnal tendencies and fancies requires solace, and solace requires forgetfulness, distraction, occupation, and entertainment

So that those elements of deception can fool the conscience and put the spirit to sleep, stopping it from feeling any pain. Otherwise, that grievous suffering scorches the conscience, the lamentation is unendurable and the anguish of despair cannot be borne.

This means, the farther one deviates from the Straight Path, the more one is stricken by this state, and the conscience cries out. Within every pleasure is a pain, which is a trace of this state.

This means that the glitter of civilization, which is a mixture of fancy, lust, amusement and dissipation, is a deceptive cure for the terrible distress that arises from misguidance; the glitter is a poisonous narcotic.

My dear friend! On our second way, that light-filled road, we perceived a state of mind in which life becomes a source of pleasure, and plain joy.

We understood that the second way imbues the spirit with a state that has various degrees according to the strength of belief. The body receives pleasure through the spirit and the spirit receives pleasure through the conscience.

An immediate pleasure is felt in the conscience; a spiritual paradise is present in the heart. Reflective thought opens up that pleasure only to increase it, while consciousness unveils secrets.

The more the heart is aroused, the more the conscience is stimulated and the spirit stirred, the greater the pleasure; fire is transformed into light and winter into summer.

The doors of paradises open up in the conscience and the world becomes a paradise. Within it our spirits take flight, soaring like falcons and kites, entreating, praying.

Dear fellow-traveler! Farewell for now. Let us offer a prayer together and then we will part to meet again!

O God! Guide us to the Straight Path. Amen.

In the Name of God, the All-Merciful, the All-Compassionate.

O the All-Merciful, O the All-Compassionate, O the All-Independent, Single One, O the All-Living, O the Self-Subsisting, O the All-Wise, O the All-Just, O the All-Holy and All-Pure!

For the sake of Your Greatest Name, and for the great merit and sacredness of the Qur'an of miraculous exposition, and for the honor of the most illustrious Messenger, upon him be peace and blessings, favor those who prepared this book for publication and published it, and all the students of the *Risale-i Nur*—the students of belief and the Qur'an—with the eternal happiness in *Jannatu'l-Firdaws*—the highest floor of Paradise. Amen! And favor them with success in the service of belief and the Qur'an. Amen! And add to their records of good deeds a thousand merits for each letter of this book—*Comparisons between Belief and Unbelief*. Amen! And favor them with patience, perseverance and utter sincerity in publishing the treatises of the *Light*. Amen! O the Most Compassionate of the compassionate! Make all the students of the *Risale-i Nur* happy in both worlds. Amen! And guard them against the evils of the satans of humankind and the jinn. Amen! And forgive the faults of this poor, helpless Said. Amen!

In the name of all the students of the *Light*,
Said Nursi

Index

Index of God's Names and Attributes